Legacy of Love

Legacy of Love

A Plan for Parenting on Purpose

Tim Kimmel

MULTNOMAH

Portland, Oregon 97266

Tim Kimmel conducts conferences for parents, corporations, and military installations on the priority of the family, and he also conducts *The Hurried Family* Seminar. For further information write or call:

Tim Kimmel
P.O. Box 31031
Phoenix, AZ 85046
(602) 996-9922

Unless otherwise indicated, all Scripture is from the New American Standard Bible, copyright The Lockman Foundation 1960, 1962, 1963, 1968, 1971, 1972, 1973, 1975, 1977. Used by permission.

Scripture quotes marked NIV are from the Holy Bible: New International Version, copyright 1973, 1978, 1984 by the International Bible Society. Used by permission of Zondervan Bible Publishers.

Cover design by Bruce DeRoos and Brenda Jose
Edited by Larry Libby and Steve Halliday

LEGACY OF LOVE
© 1989 by Tim Kimmel
Published by Multnomah Press
Portland, Oregon 97266

Multnomah Press is a ministry of Multnomah School of the Bible, 8435 N.E. Glisan Street, Portland, Oregon 97220.

Printed in the U.S.A.

Library of Congress Cataloging-in-Publication Data

Kimmel, Tim.
    Legacy of love/Tim Kimmel.
        p. cm.
    ISBN 0-88070-312-1
    1. Parenting—United States. 2. Love. 3. Parenting—Religious aspects—Christianity. 4. Values—Study and teaching—United States. 5. Family—United States—Religious Life. I. Title.
HQ755.83.K56 1989
649'.1—dc20   89-8358
                                                                 CIP

89 90 91 92 93 94 95 96 97 98 - 10 9 8 7 6 5 4 3 2

Dedication

For my father, who lives in Pennsylvania
■
And my mother, who lives in Heaven
■
Thanks for the legacy.
I'll do my best to pass it on.

Contents

Acknowledgements

No man is an island, and no book is a solo. I want to gratefully thank the following people for their contributions.

Rodger Strader: You struck the match and fanned the flames.

Larry Libby and *Steve Halliday:* Multnomah's tag team editors who flourished through the two-minute warning.

John Trent: You never stop encouraging.

Kory Schuknecht and *Barry Asmus:* For providing generous access to the think tank.

Barry and *Kay MacBan:* For getting the project moving and seeing it through. And thanks to WGM and O for the use of the catacombs.

Joe and *Judy Carlo:* For loaning me the keys to the room with the view.

Jeannie Harkey: For chasing down the details and keeping everything on course.

Mark Holmlund: You ought to rent out your mind—and your dining room table. I appreciated both.

Darcy: Your spirit lives in this book.

Karis, Cody, and *Shiloh:* The legacy is for you.

Since my youth, O God,
you have taught me,
and to this day
I declare your marvelous deeds.
Even when I am old and gray,
do not forsake me,
O God,
till I declare your power
to the next generation,
your might to all who are to come.

(Psalm 71:17-18, NIV)

Introduction

It was a bitterly cold afternoon in Washington, D.C.

I was sitting at a table in the Library of Congress, supposedly doing research for my first book.

Instead, I found myself staring without seeing at the book in front of me. I was still too stunned to study. Too sick at heart about what had happened the day before.

You remember that Tuesday. Like me, you'll probably never forget it.

The day dawned clear and cold on the East Coast. We were going about our routines, banking on the future, when the future suddenly let us down. Space shuttle shots had become so common that we barely stopped to notice them. But *that* morning we rushed to our televisions to validate the rumor.

Technology had betrayed us. Seventy-three seconds after lift-off, an O-Ring failed to maintain its seal on the seam of the solid booster rocket propelling the shuttle into space. Flames welded through the skin of the external fuel tank strapped to the bottom of the space shuttle *Challenger*. In a splinter of a second 383,000 gallons of liquid hydrogen exploded, blowing the *Challenger* into dust. Its plume of death hung in the sky long enough for the world to get a good look.

The newspeople kept showing the videotape of the seven astronauts waving as they headed for their ride into eternity. The names on their sky-blue jumpsuits would ultimately be etched in space history. *Onizuka, Jarvis, Resnik, Smith, Scobee, McNair,* and a schoolteacher named *McAuliffe.*

11

As I sat in the hard oak chair at the Library, I kept seeing Christa McAuliffe's parents standing in the VIP bleachers at Cape Canaveral. Their faces mirrored America. Pride at the prospect, anticipation at the countdown, exhilaration at the lift-off, confusion at the explosion, and then shock at the reality.

In an attempt to divert my thoughts, I decided to take a break from my reading and walk across the street to the U. S. Capitol Building. It felt good when I finally stepped out of the biting wind into the warmth of the great rotunda. I've only been in the Capitol a handful of times, but it always awes me. It's the combination of what it is and what it represents.

A small group of tourists was beginning a guided tour off to the left, so I decided to tag along. The tour guide kept up an animated cadence of statistics and anecdotes about architecture, statues, and paintings. She led us through enough halls and rooms to get us adequately turned around before ending up where we began.

Throughout the tour, our guide reeled off quips and stories that made points of interest come alive. She saved her best quip for last. Pausing a moment after her monologue, she said there was one final picture we needed to see. It was a picture of the most significant person in America.

She reached into her blazer pocket and pulled out a photo . . . of her daughter.

We all laughed, offered polite applause, and thanked her for her help. I took a closer look at her picture and then headed out the front door back toward the Library.

I hesitated at the top of the steps to take in all that had just happened. I had walked into this building in the backwash of a national tragedy. Then I'd spent some time with memories of Madison, Jefferson, Adams, Monroe, Crockett, and Webster.

Standing there on freedom's front porch, wondering about all that was going on around me, I found that a proud mom with an Olan Mills photo of her daughter made the most sense.

The space program symbolized the technology that promised to whisk us into the future—the technology that would invent solutions to all our problems. But all of technology's boasts were only as reliable as a gasket in the seam of a rocket. Technology was wonderful and helpful, but it could only carry us so far before it let us down.

The Capitol Building was a symbol of government. Built on the foundation of liberty and held up by the pillars of democracy and justice, it was an emblem of hope in a cynical world. But it couldn't deliver the future, either. Government is only as good as the conscience that motivates it. And some of the decisions from those very halls have left deep stains on our national conscience.

Standing on those wide, windswept steps, I was moved to remember that our national future doesn't rest on micro-circuits or the whims of politicians. It never has, and it never will.

Someone has stated that the true wealth of a nation is its people. I agree. But I'm inclined to narrow that definition. America's true wealth is its *parents*. They are the ones who ultimately determine whether our nation has a prayer.

Parents are the hinge on which a civilization pivots. They determine whether the door of the future swings open or closed.

But to make parenting the top priority doesn't play well in a lot of social circles. It sounds . . . exclusive somehow. As though we were saying that parents are the only ones making a contribution.

There are, of course, many factors that contribute to the strength of a civilization. But history insists that *parents* set the agenda of a culture. Their guidance—or lack of it—determines the character and longevity of a people. Because of the influence they wield, a nation is only a generation away from serious trouble. It is only as good as its moms and dads.

It sounds better in polite conversation to put children at the top of a priority list. But children aren't the wealth of a nation. They represent its greatest natural resource. They are the raw materials that a nation must use to build its destiny.

Like any natural resource, they must be mined. Skillful parents must draw out potential from the ore of imperfections.

That wouldn't be so hard if it was all we had to do. But we have planes to catch and bills to pay. We have imposed agendas that often relegate our children to some forgotten corner.

So we leave a legacy . . . but not necessarily the kind we had in mind. It takes a lot more than good intentions to leave a legacy of love. The best intentions have a tough time competing with the relentless pressures of culture. We have to be focused and strategic. Good intentions simply won't cut it.

The book you hold in your hands may represent the most strategic purchase you have made in years. Not because the book is so profound or the author is so wise. But because something nudged you to think about leaving a permanent gift to your children—a heritage that goes beyond cash and cars and property. Something moved you to think about a legacy of love *and you did something about it.*

That's the all-important first step! Now . . . with God's help . . . let's explore some ways to make that legacy the best it can be.

PART ONE

Beginning the Legacy

CHAPTER ONE

A Plan for Parenting on Purpose

It only took thirty-five seconds for the doctor to remove thirty-five years from Michael's life.

"We've isolated the reason for the occasional numbness and the excessive fatigue that you've been experiencing lately. . . ."

Twelve years of marriage was no consolation for the woman who sat next to Michael on the doctor's couch. She was hoping for the best, bracing herself for the worst. Her fingers laced with his, squeezing his hand in anticipation of the diagnosis.

"It's called amyotrophic lateral sclerosis. That's the technical term. You know this disease by another, more common name. Michael, you have Lou Gehrig's disease."

In the minutes that followed, Michael was vaguely aware of the doctor talking and his wife whimpering. But the impact of the words "Lou Gehrig's disease" cut a swath so deep in his soul that he couldn't keep his mind on events around him.

He retreated somewhere inside himself—to a refuge of air-brushed memories. He saw himself applauded by fellow employees at the announcement of his promotion to the executive wing. He saw himself marching up to take the honors for excellence at his college graduation. He saw his father leading the charge of fans onto the field after he threw the last pitch of his first and only Little League no-hitter.

The images were woven together by a common thread . . . *potential.* In one smooth stroke, that line had been severed.

Realistically, he had about three years to live. Medicine could only delay the inevitable. The facts said he had to condense a lifetime into a small parenthesis of approximately thirty-six months.

Once he accepted that reality, his focus immediately shifted from what he was losing to what he was gaining. The hand that writes the beginning and ending of our lives had given him a touch of grace. In a sad but strategic sort of way, Michael had been allowed to read the dates that would be carved on his tombstone. Because of that, he had time to do what most people don't think to do until it's too late.

He could formulate a plan to make the days count.

It took Michael only a moment to begin calculating his agenda. His first priority sat weeping next to him. She didn't bargain for this. He'd have to prepare her for the transition and maximize his moments with her. Three other items also lay on his agenda—his three children. He had to finish grooming them for the future.

From here on out, he'd have to be deliberate. That meant redefining his reason for living. Up to this point, his focus had been on carving out an economic, social, and career niche. These priorities had consumed him. Now they seemed unaffordable luxuries. Status, fame, and fortune were expensive. They exacted their tolls in *time*—large quantities of it.

God had extended Michael a timeline of credit. Now He was exercising His option to call the loan. When Michael realized how soon his most precious resource would be exhausted, he decided to invest it shrewdly. The days had to count—every one of them. Financial legacies could be squandered. Legacies of fame quickly forgotten. The one thing that could survive beyond his life was a legacy of love.

Limited Time

Michael's dilemma points to the kernel issue of life. Why is it that we don't realize how valuable time is until we've run out of it?

Desperation moves our focus from wants to needs, from desires to necessities. When the props are pulled away, we quickly see what really matters. And what really matters are relationships. People.

Such stories of dying men reveal what all of us need to see—but can't because of the cultural distractions. When we read about an ordinary person who learns he has but three years to live, we can't help but put ourselves into the scenario. What if it were me? How would I feel?

Let me bring this close to home by suggesting that it *is* you! And me. God regularly reminds us that we live on a fixed amount of time—but we are too caught up in what we are doing to see it. He tells us:

"You only have ten years left to imprint this boy with the character he needs to survive the future."

"In two years this daughter will be taking her cues from her boyfriend. Prepare her now to be wise then!"

"In five minutes this boy is going to walk away from this incident. You will never again have an opportunity quite like this to show him how proud you are."

Sometimes He whispers to you as you're walking through the family room and you see your eight-year-old daughter asleep on the couch. You notice that her body now stretches the length of the sofa and you remember that it was *only yesterday* when she could be cradled in the bend of your arm. He speaks to you when you see your teenaged son plowing through a stack of philosophy books, trying desperately to draw some conclusions about life. He shouts at you when you pack the car for a family vacation and nobody wants to go with you anymore.

These deadlines come and go every day. Too many are ignored either because we are distracted by competition from our rat race lifestyle, or we simply don't know how to seize the moment.

That's why we need a plan.

A plan means we're deliberate. And deliberate is a concept whose time has come. Maintaining our competitive edge in this "Age of Information" requires that we work from a clearly defined strategy.

We do fairly well at things which can be easily measured: the goal line, the waistline, the deadline, the bottom line. But when it comes to something as abstract as people, we grope. We stumble.

It's understandable why we allow things like jobs to take priority over family. Career responsibilities are easier to define, superior/subordinate relationships are non-negotiable, and success can be measured on payday.

Family members, on the other hand, are unpredictable. Fragile. They entertain unrealistic expectations, undefined hopes, and Mount Everest-size fears. When it comes to relationships that last a lifetime, our culture embraces a trial-and-error, shoot-from-the-hip attitude. We know that we should be as deliberate at home as we are everywhere else, but we can't seem to figure out how. And our inconsistency leaves us feeling guilty.

Portrait or Collage?

If you could portray your family in "the ideal setting," what setting would you choose? I know the answer for me: the small-town pathos of a Norman Rockwell print. If anyone captured the concept of a loving legacy, he did. I was speaking near his hometown of Stockbridge, Massachusetts one winter and visited the museum that contains the largest collection of his original works. As I moved from room to room, I stood inches away from the masterpieces that have stirred the hearts of the world.

Many things could be said about Rockwell's work, but one thing stands out: family. Family formed the backdrop of his art. Although he depicted people in myriad settings, they were never far from their roots. Family wasn't a compartment of life, it was always "the big picture." Whether it was a grandfather taking his grandson fishing, a couple applying for a marriage license, a young soldier being welcomed home by a neighborhood, a girl torn between childhood and adulthood as she gazes in a mirror, or an extended family sitting around the Thanksgiving table, the theme was clear. No matter where you are, no matter who you are, you need to belong to a family.

Not long after I returned from Stockbridge, we received a Christmas card from a family we knew fairly well. The card featured a Rockwell Christmas scene on the cover. Inside they had a picture of their own family. But instead of enclosing a family portrait by the Christmas tree, they had pasted together snapshots of each family member in a collage. I knew this family well enough to know that they hadn't chosen that form of family photo for effect, but rather for convenience. Their kids were going so many directions and Dad and Mom had such crowded schedules that it was impossible to assemble everyone at one spot long enough to press the shutter.

Their family life was a mishmash of moments clipped from disjointed schedules. The outside of the card was Norman Rockwell, but the inside looked like a Picasso.

Most people want life to be different . . . but don't think they can do anything to change "the way they are." They want to leave a legacy of love—a legacy that never dies—but assume it's too late. I have yet to meet a mom and dad who don't love their children. Although some parents struggle, deep down they want to imprint their children with qualities and character traits that can stand the test of time.

They simply get bogged down in the rat race.

Men are too busy competing in the work arena. They rationalize their failures by thinking lame, macho thoughts. They try to relegate all this dreamy talk about babies and children to women. Besides, they've got their work cut out for them. If they stop long enough to rock the kid or read him a book, their competition might have them for lunch.

Meanwhile, the women are passing the men on the ladder to the top. Mom is punching the clock at the office, while the children are punching the clock at the day-care center.

This reminds me of a story I learned in school about life in the California Gold Rush days. Miners slaved in the hot sun day after day. They'd swirl sand around in their pans for hours to extract tiny glimmers of gold. Most of what they ended up with was "gold dust."

But it had value. Supplies at the general store and whiskey in the saloons could be had simply by sprinkling a little bit of that dust on a scale. Sometimes, however, just as they poured the stuff, someone opened a door and allowed a gust of wind to blow some particles off the scale—where they would settle through the cracks in the floor. At other times the miners were simply careless. In their hurry to get what they wanted, they'd sacrifice more of their precious gold than they needed to. It would float through the air . . . and ultimately slip through the cracks.

Our relationship to our kids has too often followed similar lines. We've had an economic surge at the end of the twentieth century that has placed serious pressure on our children, and the demands of our high-tech/information economy have made it too easy for precious moments with our children to slip through the cracks.

We are called to steward our kids, to groom them for the future. Their minds are blank slates. Their characters are moldable clay. When they are young, they want to imitate us, to worship us.

But the professional world draws and rivets our attention. We collectively spend billions on ads, psychological profiles, and demographic studies so that we may woo, wow, and win our clients. Meanwhile, back at the condominium, a few extremely impressionable souls just wait to be programmed.

Distracted parents miss opportunities—the "little things" that happen day to day that provide the chance to leave a legacy of love. We miss the chance . . .

. . . to hear a child's first words

. . . to watch the baby's first step

. . . to follow up with discipline when the child is caught in a lie, thus teaching an on-the-spot lesson in honesty

. . . to run by the bike when the child first sheds training wheels

. . . to hear about the first date, the first kiss

. . . to drop a powerful seed-thought into the fertile soil of a teachable moment; profound moments that are few and far between in a lifetime.

These things fall through the proverbial "cracks" in our lives, and we miss them. The solution isn't to patch the cracks—you can never do that. The cracks are there, part of any day.

The solution is to handle the gold more carefully. Gold is valuable because it's rare—just like these opportunities to influence our children. Time can be my enemy or my ally. If I don't treat it with the respect it demands, it will rob me of my greatest possessions.

Two Fathers, Two Legacies

Two young men, value-programmed in the same decades and raised in similar lifestyles of affluence, demonstrate the tragic difference between opportunities handled carefully and opportunities lost. Meet Jeff and Mark.

Jeff was twenty-eight and felt imprisoned. The bondage he wanted to escape was homosexuality. Here had been a young boy trying desperately to win the attention of his father. Jeff's dad was a wealthy, successful businessman who worked a lot of evenings and most weekends. He manipulated Jeff with false promises and kept him out of his hair with empty pledges.

He promised Jeff a lot of things, but his most worn-out assurance was that he would take him fishing. Plans would be made at the beginning of a week only to be dashed at the last minute by something "urgent" or "more important" at the office.

Finally the day arrived. Jeff's dad shook him awake before dawn on Saturday morning. They ate a big breakfast, got the tackle box and poles packed, and took off . . . to a trout "farm" on the edge of town.

There was no drive through the country, no father-and-son talks by a quiet lake, no lectures on patience, no shared picnic lunch, no boy falling asleep on his father's lap on the way home. Just a small tank filled with starved fish. They caught their limit in fifteen minutes. His dad let the "professionals" clean them there. They were home barely an hour after they had left, and Jeff's father tore out the driveway to get in a full day at the office.

Jeff remembers that day as if it were yesterday. "It was the greatest hour of my life, and it was the worst hour of my life. When I saw my dad driving off for his office, I knew that I was nothing more than an inconvenience to his schedule."

What a contrast is Mark's story. He, too, grew up in a wealthy home with an aggressive businessman father. But all similarities ended there. Mark's father never let the demands of success and his duties as provider keep him from spending large chunks of time with his son. He taught him truth, helped him apply it wisely, and gave him safe boundaries of discipline.

I ran into Mark last week at a social function. A couple of us were chatting with him about the pressures that a volatile economy put upon people like his dad. He admitted the economy had been tough on his father, but he said, "I just hope I can turn out to be as great a man as he is." Here was a thirty-year-old man still hoping to emulate his good father.

Mark has been given a legacy of love. He will pass it on to his children, and they will pass it on to theirs. That's the thing about a legacy of love: It just keeps coming back generation after generation.

You may be a parent with small children, or your children may be heading into adulthood. One thing I can assure you is that it is never too late. You may have twenty years, or like Michael at the beginning of the chapter, only three. But you can still make an impact, a significant one.

If someone gave you a peek at the last page in the story of your life, and you realized you only had three years to live, could you make a strategic difference in the lives of your children? I want to suggest that it is not only possible, it's biblical.

I'm thinking of someone else who found Himself with only three years to live. He had some convictions He wanted to instill in a rag-tag group of men around Him. He was confident that if He did His job well, they would pass on those convictions. He didn't have the benefit of a library of self-help books. He didn't get to utilize the "grapevine" of a global communications network. Although He maintained a crowded daily schedule, His work never got in the way of His mission. He wanted to pass on a legacy of love to a handful of close friends.

Three years were all He had. But He accomplished His mission. When they lowered His lifeless body from the cross, His enemies thought it was over. But it was just beginning. Before they had time to carve in the date of His death, He vacated His tomb, leaving it behind as a monument to His deity. Twenty centuries later, the entire world enjoys the benefits of this unique Man who knew how to leave a legacy of love.

The good news is that He left footprints. Let's follow them and see where they lead. . . .

CHAPTER TWO

A Blueprint for Your Child's Character

My secretary slipped into the office with a phone message. The word *urgent* was circled and underlined.

It's ironic how problems that have been years in the making become urgent when the consequences of neglect suddenly materialize. I knew the man who had left the message. The warning light on the dashboard of his conscience had been glowing for years. My guess was that the things he'd been warned about were finally coming true.

I dialed his number. His secretary asked if I could meet him at his office and then leave for lunch from there. I had a feeling that the lunch was merely a bribe that kept him from having to leave his own turf. But it *was* lunchtime, and I *was* hungry.

She ushered me into his cluttered office. He was a builder by trade and kept in touch with most of his customers by telephone. That explained why he was on the phone as I entered the room. He continued to talk for the next ten minutes while I waited. There was something strangely consistent about what I was seeing. Whenever I thought of him, I always pictured a man on the telephone . . . like it was part of his head.

When he finally hung up, I figured we'd open with a few minutes of small talk. But that wasn't to be. Tears welled up in his eyes and anger rose in his voice as he described his son, his two daughters, and his wife. His children, spread over a six year span, were now teenagers. He felt he should be getting combat pay. His wife, he complained, was the infant of the family and conspired with the kids to plot his first visit to a cardiac care unit.

I grew embarrassed as I watched this grown man sputter out angry words of frustration and bitterness. The kids, the wife. The wife, the kids. They were a mess and they were driving him over the edge.

Soon he described why he'd called me. One of his daughters had teamed up with a wayward young man and had committed a felony. A legal firm was handling their problems with the state, but he hoped I might be able to help his daughter solve the moral nightmare that had created this mess.

He was trying to subcontract his family problems to me.

There's no magic wand in my pocket, and, frankly, situations as complicated as this require a whole lot more attention than I normally have time to give. But I didn't want to leave it at that. He was hurting and I wanted to help. Still, it seemed so uphill.

I asked what he had done so far, and what he planned to do. His answers: "Nothing" and "I don't know." My questions could have encompassed his whole career as a father and the answers would have been the same. But maybe it wasn't so surprising: *his* father's track record bore similar statistics.

I was desperate for a way to show this man, my friend, that nothing he might do would have any lasting effect until he established a plan that considered the unique needs of his children's lives from start to finish. I knew I needed an object lesson—something that works when simple words fall flat.

That's when the Lord opened my eyes to an illustration right under my nose. The man was a builder; in fact, he was an excellent builder. His office was cluttered with blueprints.

I grabbed one.

I set it down on his desk, spread it out, flipped through a few pages, and then asked:

"What comes first, the building or the blueprints?"

The answer barely required a Romper Room IQ, but some of the most important things in life are built on simple principles. He gave me the obvious response.

"You wouldn't think of dumping a lot of building materials at a construction site and then giving the subcontractors the freedom to put them where they think they looked and worked the best, would you?" I asked. He answered on cue.

I pointed to a page of blueprints devoted to the foundation; another to the roof; another to the walls; another to the windows and doors; still another to the electricity, plumbing, heating, and insulation. Everything about the building was designed in advance. Its form and function, its profile and purpose were predetermined in the blueprints.

"Have you developed a set of blueprints for your children's character?" I asked. "What's the foundation on which you're structuring their lives? Have you picked out the best windows and doors for them to access the outside world, capture the view, and benefit from the Light of the World? Have you factored in the proper insulation to protect them from life's dangerous elements, and attached them to the right kind of power to light them for a lifetime?

Er . . . well . . . he *had* taken them to church and enrolled them in Christian schools since kindergarten.

I suggested that the church and Christian school had probably done their parts well. But *he* was the contractor. They were only subcontractors. They merely helped him put together what God had ordained *him* to build.

It was obvious that he and his wife had not determined much of anything in advance. They didn't have a blueprint for their kids, their marriage, or their personal lives. Yet he wouldn't think of erecting a building without a predetermined set of plans. If he had applied the principles that he used for building a structure to building *people,* he wouldn't have found himself in such a mess. Now he was forced to do some demolition and restructuring which would demand heavy commitments of time, energy, and resources from all involved.

It wasn't too late. But it was going to be emotionally expensive.

You Can Run, but You Can't Hide

If a minister wants to make his congregation squirm and look at their watches more than usual, all he has to do is quote one particular verse from the Bible. It's one of those verses whose cold wind makes your conscience shiver.

It's securely wedged in the Ten Commandments—just between numbers two and three. And like everything else in the Scriptures, it wasn't put there by accident. God's talking to Moses when He says:

> . . . I, the LORD your God, am a jealous God,
> visiting the iniquity of the fathers on the children,
> on the third and the fourth generations of those
> who hate Me (Exodus 20:5).

Hearing a verse like this puts some people on the defensive. They want to dismiss it as folklore. The concept of inherited judgment just doesn't suit our modern sensibilities.

Others, unwilling to play games with the Scriptures, sense impending defeat. They think of the grand flaws of their own parents and assume they're doomed. Nor do they have to reflect long to figure out the kind of curse they may be creating for their own children.

Nevertheless, the truth of this verse stands. Counselors, psychologists, social workers, ministers, and police officers consistently use childhood studies to explain a person's behavior. If our father was undemonstrative, we may have difficulty showing our affections. If our parents kept two sets of books, we're more inclined to. Some sins have a moral half-life that keeps them lingering indefinitely. Child molesting is one type of sin that keeps raising its ugly head generation after generation.

We see a nasty picture of "generational sin" in the Old Testament. While Moses received the Ten Commandments atop the stormy heights of Mount Sinai, a fickle congregation played down in the valley. This restless generation of parents would be the first to feel the teeth of the divine curse. They pushed their patient and long-suffering God one time too many. And then He showed them that He wasn't kidding. In Numbers 14:31-33, God outlines the result of their rebellion:

> Your children, however, whom you said would
> become a prey—I will bring them in, and they
> shall know the land which you have rejected.

31

But as for you, your corpses shall fall in this wilderness. And your sons shall be shepherds for forty years in the wilderness, and they shall suffer for your unfaithfulness, until your corpses lie in the wilderness.

True to His Word, God dealt with this unfaithful generation. And for the next forty years, children buried their parents.

This curse makes sense when you see it in its context. God demands to be the leader of our lives. He makes clear that He will not share that position with anything or anybody. As our Creator, He knows our strengths and weaknesses—He knows where we are safe, and where we are endangered. That's why the second commandment forbids us to embrace idols of any kind. Idolatry is the kiss of death to the family. It afflicted the generation at Sinai, and it afflicts generations today. That's why God was emphatic about the consequences of unbelief and idolatry.

A Long Walk in the Right Direction

While it's true that ministers can sometimes ruin our day by quoting Exodus 20:5, don't forget that verse 5 isn't God's final word on the subject. The curse for those who disobey is followed by a promise for those who choose to trust God and walk in obedience to His Word. Put on your glasses and read the fine print in verse 6 . . .

But showing lovingkindness to thousands, to those who love Me and keep My commandments.

I like the way God developed this same thought in Deuteronomy 7:9:

Know therefore that the LORD your God, He is God, the faithful God, who keeps His covenant and His lovingkindness to a thousandth generation with those who love Him and keep His commandments.

Unfaithfulness can haunt a family for three to four generations. But righteousness can reward it indefinitely.

So why don't average people in the pew respond to the promise? It's because they're already overwhelmed by the curse. They can point so easily to so many negatives in their life that they assume their situation is hopeless. Like my friend lacking a blueprint for his children, many feel the situation is beyond repair.

The New Testament gives hope for our dismal situation. Paul wrote two letters to a group which had raised idolatry to an art form—and which had consequently suffered the consequences for generations. Here is what he wrote:

> Therefore if any man is in Christ, he is a new creature; the old things passed away; behold, new things have come (2 Corinthians 5:17).

If man's greatest need had been knowledge, God would have sent us an educator.

If man's greatest need had been physical health, God would have sent us a doctor.

If man's greatest need had been money, God would have sent us an entrepreneur.

If man's greatest need had been excitement, God would have sent us an entertainer.

But man's greatest need was forgiveness, so God sent us a Savior.

A relationship with that Savior can preempt the curse of disobedience. God's grace can free us from the oppression of our childhood and give us direction for our own responsibilities as parents.

Anticipating Needs

To leave a legacy of love we need to ask the right questions long before we need the answers. Just as an auto manufacturer tries to anticipate every problem a particular vehicle might have before he puts someone behind the wheel, we need to think ahead and imagine what kind of adults we want our children to become.

I cut my ministry eyeteeth working with teenagers. There's something about the nature of young people that forces youth workers to focus on fundamentals. They want solutions that aren't steeped in theory. And they have a high capacity to make sacrificial adjustments to their lives when they are convinced of what's true.

The process of discipleship and the process of parenting share some common denominators. We are to nurture our children so that when they step into the future, they'll be equipped for its demands.

That's why serious youth workers disciple with a finished product in mind. That's exactly what we need to do as parents. We need to profile our children *in advance*, anticipating their needs and maintaining a clear idea of what they will be like once they're on their own.

A Checklist for My Child's Future

As a youth worker, I found that five points of emphasis were all I needed to tailor-make a strategy for building a kid into a mature adult. The checklist also serves as an excellent confidence builder and can become a blueprint to independence. Let's look at the following points with our own children in mind.

When my children move out from under my authority they need . . .

Decision-making skills:

In physical issues: exercise, nutrition, rest, etc.

In personal issues: finances, career, home life, etc.

In social issues: dating relationships, love, friendships, dealing with enemies, etc.

In spiritual issues: dealing with sin, faith, prayer, fellowship, etc.

Character traits:

Faith, Integrity, Poise, Discipline, Endurance, and Courage.

Commitment to life goals:

To love and obey God.

To love their spouse.

To love their children.

To be a good friend.

To work hard.

To invest their lives in others.

Ability to execute survival skills:

In the physical: manage a schedule, cook, swim, learn safety skills, drive, etc.

In the personal: live on a budget, manage a checkbook, know how to finish projects, keep belongings maintained, etc.

In the social: get along with others, confront, resolve, employ good manners, learn to stand alone if necessary, etc.

In the spiritual: share their faith, repent, be a friend of God, etc.

Sustained relationships:

Ability to resolve conflict, serve others, communicate, listen, forgive, etc.

This list isn't the last word on the characteristics and skills we need to transfer to our children, but it can give you some ideas. By using the five areas in this checklist, we can develop an individual profile or blueprint for each one of our children and enhance it as he or she grows older.

These confidence builders have a "one-size-fits-all" character. Most of your responses to this checklist probably apply to all of your children. At the same time these five statements allow us to consider the uniqueness of each child.

For instance, you may have a son that has a learning disability while his sister is a scholar. The kinds of skills you expect your son to master might be quite different from those you ask of your daughter. Gender should also be considered in the blueprint; the responsibilities of a young man on a date are different from those of a girl. Or you may have a child that excels in sports and will therefore wish to design his or her profile with that in mind.

The point is, leaving a legacy of love demands that we have a clear idea of what's required. Developing a blueprint for the finished product puts us miles ahead.

Benefits of the Blueprint

Obvious benefits come with knowing in advance the kind of adults we want to create out of the raw materials that live under our roofs.

Anxiety is often the result of confusion. People can't figure out who they are, what they are trying to accomplish, or where they are heading. We're guaranteed a restless heart if we try to take our cues from a confused culture.

Nothing intimidates us quite like our responsibilities as parents. The thought that our inadequacies could cause the permanent downfall of our children can rob us of the joy of parenthood. By having a strategy for developing our children's character, we release our spirits from the bondage of fear. We can rest in the fact that we see the big picture—even while we struggle with the day-to-day challenges that come from overseeing a family.

This doesn't mean we won't have problems. Problems are an inescapable part of the parenting landscape. But the backdrop of the "big picture" keeps us from falling apart when particular events don't play out the way we'd like.

My purpose is clearer

We can enjoy our parenting years when we have a target and when, each year, we get better at aiming our children toward it. The psalmist compared children to arrows. He said, "Blessed is the man whose quiver is full." Proverbs 22:6 gets a lot of pulpit time throughout the world. It states:

> Train up a child in the way he should go, even when he is old he will not depart from it.

"In the way he should go . . ." literally means "according to his inner bent." The expression has its roots in the idea of a bent bow ready to shoot an arrow. A tailor-made blueprint for each of my children forces me to discover their inner bents, to study the unique qualities and characteristics that make each of them an individual of great potential. Knowing this clarifies my purpose as a parent. It keeps me from being badgered by worldly philosophies.

My children are confident

Parents who have a balanced and defined purpose for their children can more effectively articulate what they expect of their children. When children know the skills they need to perfect—the decision-making abilities that maturity demands, the spiritual tools needed to maintain faith, and the relational expertise needed to live in harmony with others—they feel better about their struggles. When they know that their parents are conscientious and deliberate about their welfare, they are more inclined to cooperate. They are capable of developing deeper confidence in their parents' leadership.

My strategy is complete

A blueprint for my child's character keeps me from wondering, "What should I be doing now or next?" I know what needs to be in place by the time my child moves out from under my authority.

For example, our children need to know how to handle money. I don't need to wonder *if* they should have an allowance, but *when;* not *if* they should get a checking account, but *when;* not *if* they should have to generate income in order to learn how to handle it, but *how.* With a blueprint, we see all the ingredients necessary for building a balanced character. It's a family template that helps us make the hard decisions.

My priorities are challenged

A blueprint for our children's character not only serves them well, but also helps to evaluate our own lives. Kids don't buy the theoretical. They are firm converts to the seeing-is-believing school of thought, and if they see us preaching one thing and practicing another, they'll call us on it. Count on it.

My child's future requires me to make careful choices *now.* I can't enjoy the luxury of pursuing my desires and dreams at the expense of my family.

I know that's not always easy. We live in a culture which preaches that true value can only be measured in dollars and cents, in hood ornaments and designer labels. Success—that great god of the marketplace—demands worship at the expense of people, who live forever. When will we realize that such "success" is a deadly fantasy?

A legacy of love demands that I submit my personal ambitions to the greater needs of my family—and that's impossible if I swallow the world's line about success. It is for that reason Darcy and I have redefined success in line with our higher calling as parents. We define it this way:

SUCCESS:

THE CONSCIENTIOUS STEWARDING

OF THE

NEXT GENERATION

Two Profiles

The Wall Street Journal, which likes to call itself the "Bible of the business world," featured a front-page article on one of the greatest athletes ever to wear Dodger Blue.

Orel Hershiser was the most valuable player of the 1988 World Series. The Los Angeles Dodgers met the highly favored Oakland A's for the fall classic. Though most of the "smart money" was riding on the Oakland squad, the A's never really threatened. One big reason for that was the way Hershiser dominated the second and last games of the series. He put on a pitching clinic that left the opposing leadoff hitters shaking their heads and made the rest of the order wish they weren't on national TV.

When Hershiser puts on the spikes and slips his hand in the glove, he's the best of the best. And when he puts on a business suit he's as shrewd as they come. But the man inside the man has a higher calling than baseball or the wealth it's brought. He loves the Lord Jesus Christ with all of his heart.

That same *Wall Street Journal* article outlined Hershiser's conservative strategy for protecting his wealth.

It made it clear that this athlete's money and his career were being kept in submission to his responsibilities as a Christian. Listen to the article:

> But money is only part of the equation for success, Mr. Hershiser says. He says that his attorney once suggested he ask himself several questions every time he wanted to assess his major league career: Am I still married? Are my children happy, and do they know me? Do I still have my friends? If you can answer yes to these questions, then you are having a great career.[1]

About a week after this article was published, another world-class baseball player made the news.

Pete Rose has been a synonym for aggressive baseball ever since he put on a Cincinnati Reds uniform. He so won the affection of that town that it named the street to Riverfront Stadium after him. He's been an Ohio icon for over a decade. Why? He amassed more base hits than any player in history. He hit with a vengeance, ran with a vengeance, slid with a vengeance, and even occasionally struck out with a vengeance.

Unfortunately, he may also have gambled with a vengeance. At this writing he finds himself under scrutiny for betting on baseball games (which is strictly forbidden and grounds for permanent suspension from baseball).

In the process of getting the story on Rose, some reporters decided to interview family members to find out what kind of man lived behind the image.

A front-page lead article in *USA Today* outlined a man in sharp contrast to Orel Hershiser. Listen to what the daughter of Pete Rose said:

> [He's] the world's worst father. I will never understand why he never had any time for us. We didn't expect anything from him, except to just like us.

The day after the article came out someone asked Rose about his daughter's comments. "I don't know what she's complaining about," he said, "I bought her a new Mercedes last week."

Rose's son, Pete II, recounted how he had been prevented from telephoning his dad.

> Even if I wanted to call him, I don't have his telephone number. I have to call his agent, and he tells my dad I want to talk to him. We don't get in touch unless my dad wants to. Still, I love him. He's my dad.[2]

Two men in baseball uniforms. One is on his way to becoming a metaphor for integrity. The other has already become a metaphor for folly. One had a plan, the other didn't have a prayer.

How about you? If *USA Today* were to interview your kids twenty years from now about your own parenting legacy, what would they say? Would the kids find comfort and pleasure in their memories? Or would they admit they didn't even have your phone number?

The choice is yours. And you make it when you answer one simple question:

Do you have a plan for building your children's character?

When it comes to parenting, you can't afford to strike out.

PART TWO

Building the Legacy

CHAPTER THREE

Building Blocks

Most people thought they were a twenty-first-century family with the world by the tail.

He was an attorney for the Phoenix branch of a large New York conglomerate. His wife was a highly paid legal assistant he had met through his work. Because of the substantial income they both enjoyed, their friends assumed their marriage was a merger made in heaven. How could they lose with such a head start?

His schedule had him shuttling between New York and Phoenix. Two weeks home, two weeks away. That nets out to six months at home per year. She, although based in Phoenix, had a far more complicated schedule that seldom found her at home. Work got the largest blocks of her time. She split the remainder between aerobics, art classes, piano, and her weekly stretch on the ballet bar.

Somehow these two ships passed in the night long enough to conceive a little dinghy. During the pregnancy, this highly educated, age-of-information couple devoured all the standard books on parenting read by the typical, upwardly-mobile secular parents-to-be. By the time their baby girl arrived, they had all the players in position.

Their strategy was simple: Maintain business as usual, and make sure the baby had the best care that money could buy.

It wasn't long until the little girl's calendar started to look as crowded and complicated as her parents'. Within days after the birth, the mother was in her three-piece suit at the word processor, in her leotards at aerobics, in her smock at art class, and in her tutu at ballet lessons. Someone stayed with the daughter until she was walking and talking. Then she was handed over to professionals. Her typical week started with reading readiness and pre-K computer classes each morning. The afternoon schedule featured gymboree Monday, piano Tuesday, ballet Wednesday, drama Thursday, and tap on Friday. Two nights a week and all Saturday morning found her on the soccer field or T-ball diamond. She went to church on the traditional holidays and spent an hour each month with a child psychologist.

Everything went according to schedule until shortly after her sixth birthday . . . when she started her menstrual cycle.

The father thought it odd, but felt no sense of urgency.

The mother assumed her girl was growing up a little faster than other girls and looked on it with a sense of quiet pride. I found their response to these circumstances chilling.

The doctors who dealt with the first-grader arrived at another conclusion. First they determined there was nothing fundamentally wrong with her system that would cause this normally adolescent phenomenon to occur so early.

Next they began to focus on the little girl's schedule—and a disturbing consensus emerged. She was indeed growing up fast. Too fast. She was completely stressed, and her body was reacting to the pressure.

Our emotional system can be compared to the circuit breakers that guard the electrical systems in our house. When a circuit overloads, the breaker pops in order to avoid a fire or a meltdown in the wiring. When our emotional system gets overloaded, our emotional circuit breakers pop. Tears are a natural and often healthy way our system deals with stress. But there are a host of problems that, when experienced in extreme or prolonged ways, can signal a serious overload to the system. That's what this girl's premature menstrual cycle represented.

What she needed was a strategy less geared to making her a clone of her parents and more geared to building her a foundation of love and confidence. She didn't have the sophisticated emotional and physical makeup required to maintain the kind of schedule her parents had arranged for her.

Yes, the professionals these parents had hired were arguably blue ribbon. You couldn't buy any better supervision and instruction. But this couple had a hard lesson to learn: *You can't pay anybody to love your kids!*

We can pay people to watch them, teach them, train them, play with them, and protect them. But we cannot hand a person money and instruct him or her to love our children. Love comes from the heart, not the checkbook.

All of the programs designed to hone your child's body and mind are nothing without a plan to build up his or her sense of confidence through a secure and binding love with Mom and Dad.

This is a task that cannot be delegated.

If success for a parent is the conscientious stewarding of the next generation, we need a blueprint for our children's heart and soul as well as their mind and body. There is no way that we can consider sending them into adulthood without equipping them in all the dimensions of life.

Considering today's high-powered competition for a child's values, a serious parent can live with a burdened heart—or a relaxed one. What determines whether we endure or enjoy our position as parents is the way we approach the *inside* of our children's lives. If we know what they need, and the character traits that we must transfer to them, we can enjoy a higher level of confidence in our responsibilities as parents.

In the next six chapters, I want to discuss six building blocks that will enable us to leave a legacy of love. These are skills for living that, once transferred, infuse our children with calm assurance—and take the fear out of tomorrow.

CHAPTER FOUR

Faith

The buttons on my car radio keep me tuned to several Phoenix "nostalgia" stations. Nostalgia is a nice word for music that's been on the classic charts for decades. They play the hits that were popular when I was a kid, but the way they keep introducing them as "relics from the past" makes me want to stop by the station and poke the young DJ with my cane.

Actually, I'm not that old. But then again, I'm not that young. I'm not ready for Geritol in an IV bottle, but I've got to admit that with each passing year the days of my childhood become more bronzed in my memory. That's probably why the songs of the '50s and '60s mean so much to me. A few bars of the Beatles and I'm back in my tie-dyed T-shirt and bell-bottomed jeans.

I was slipping through traffic a couple of days ago when the DJ spun an old Drifters number that drew me into a wistful time warp. You know the one I'm talking about. It was the song of escape and solace for anyone stuck in the steamy, concrete confines of the city. They sang . . .

When this old world starts getting me down,
And people are just too much for me to take.
I climb way up to the top of the stairs,
And all my cares just drift right into space

On the roof's the only place I know,
Where you just have to wish to make it so . . .
Up on the roof.[3]

I doubt the Drifters had some great theological truth in mind when they recorded that cut, but my imagination doesn't have to drift very far to see one. Cities are monuments to the people who built them. Skyscrapers tower over the rank-and-file folks who work and play in their shadows. They feel the suffocating pressure as their man-made world cages them in.

But if you know the right door, and you're willing to climb enough stairs, you can break into the crisp, sweet freedom of the night sky. Lying back on the roof you can stare into the middle of space. You can see beyond the asphalt jungle and look over the heads of surrounding skyscrapers. The infinite expanse puts man and his machines in a different light.

I grew up in rural America. I didn't have to take the elevator to get away from the crush. What's more, I didn't have to go anywhere to be reminded of the awesome Creator who offers me escape.

That's because I was raised in a loving home, with parents who recognized the importance of a spiritual life. Early on, I came to know and love the God who lived within my parents.

You can't transfer a legacy of love to your child if you ignore the issue of faith. Faith enables us to see the big picture, to enjoy the God who was there before we were born and who will exist forever after we've gone. Without faith, a person cannot enjoy true confidence. Without faith, a person cannot embrace truth.

But truth is a word that prompts debate. Because there is no way to pin down truth's absolutes within the strict boundaries of the scientific method, many people assume that it is beyond us. Unknowable. Unreachable.

Without faith, a child grows up under a shadow, unsure, never free, unprotected. And Mom and Dad's token nods to God on Christmas and Easter only complicate the confusion.

Children are born with a gaping emptiness in their souls, put there by the God who made them so they might recognize their need for Him. The person without God can feel the void.

If the void isn't filled with God's presence, the powers of darkness are more than happy to fill it with substitutes. Self, work, accomplishments, anger, drugs, and sex build shrines in the hearts of those who lack the personal presence of God.

Three Huge Problems

Kids look so "perfect" in the maternity ward. Unfortunately, the hospital requires us to take them home! That sheen of perfection wears through in a hurry.

All children are born with three huge problems only God can solve. These three problems are bigger than your child's personal ability to solve them. Even without the words needed to articulate the problems, a child senses them early on . . . and gropes for solutions.

Problem #1: I am an enemy of God

Children are born without a relationship with God. Although they are candidates to receive His mercy and grace, they will ultimately be judged by the absolute standards of His holiness. On their own, they can do nothing to change their position.

Problem #2: I am a slave to sin

I don't know when you discovered your child had a sin nature, but we saw it in one of ours even before we left the hospital. When Darcy tried to give Cody his first drink of Mom's milk, he stiffened his little body until it went rigid. He didn't *want* to eat yet. But when his first trip to the bar was through and Darcy pulled him away, Cody screamed bloody murder. He wasn't *ready* to finish yet.

Whenever I hear some misguided person discuss the cherubic nature of children, I have to laugh. They obviously haven't had any. Don't get me wrong—life around the Kimmel house isn't made up of wars or rumors of wars. For the most part, we enjoy a peaceful co-existence as a family. But that old sin nature is always there . . . just below the surface of the conversation, just behind the smile, just within striking distance of the most sublime moment. Nor does it isolate its efforts on the children! It haunts their parents with equal vengeance.

Left unresolved, the problem of sin can destroy a person. A legacy of love demands that this problem be acknowledged and overcome.

Problem #3: I must die

The Grim Reaper shadows our children from the delivery room to the mortuary. No one, short of those living in the final generation, will be spared his scythe.

Children learn of their finiteness early in life. Some parents try to insulate them from the certainty of death. But eventually the kids figure it out.

And they should.

Hiding from death by failing to look at it is as foolish as a child covering his eyes and assuming that, because he can't see you, you aren't there.

Death is inescapable. No matter how hard you try to deflect or delay it, it ultimately gets its way.

I'm reminded of a certain wealthy merchant of Baghdad who employed a young servant. The boy was a cut above the competition, reliable beyond his years, and enjoyed the favor and confidence of his master.

One morning the servant boy was in the marketplace doing some buying for his master when something brushed up against him. He spun around and saw the woman Death. She appeared to make threatening gestures at him and he shrank from her in cold fear.

He ran home to his master and blurted out the events.

"I was in the market doing some buying when something brushed up against me. When I turned, I saw the woman Death, and she made threatening gestures at me. If you let me borrow your fastest horse and I left immediately, I could be in Sumaria by tonight."

The master granted the boy's wish, and the lad galloped off in a blur.

Later that day, the master was in the marketplace and saw the woman Death. He approached her.

"My most trusted servant was here this morning working for me when something brushed up against him. When he turned around he saw you, and he said that you made threatening gestures at him."

Death replied, "It wasn't threatening gestures, but a look of surprise that he saw. I was so surprised to see him here this morning because I have an appointment with him tonight . . . in Sumaria."

Children learn of death, the enemy, in the day-to-day changes of nature. I've been feuding with some Arizona sparrows ever since we moved into our house. In late winter I see the mother sparrows snooping around the overhangs and soffits of our house. No matter how hard I try to eliminate their options, they always manage to find two or three spots to build their nests.

Don't misunderstand. I'm not against birds, or birds having birds. But invariably, one or two of the young sparrows fall from their nest. If the impact of the concrete doesn't send them to that big nest in the sky, my Florence Nightingale daughter will. Her intentions are divine, but she hasn't saved one yet. Her TLC is too much for their feeble lives. And when they die, our daughter falls apart. This girl could be a professional mourner. There are viewing hours, matchbox caskets, graveside services, and lots of tears.

I'm not certain whether it's a unique difference between boys and girls, or just the personality differences between Karis and Cody. But my son views death with a stiffer set of nerves.

Cody had two fish, Bartyles and Jaymes (both had a serious drinking problem). One night I was getting Cody ready for bed when I noticed that one of his fish had died. (I think it was Ed.) When I told him, I could see that he was sad. But he was determined to be brave and face the death head-on.

I asked him if he wanted to bury the fish at sea. He did. So we went into the bathroom and laid Ed to rest in the appropriate place. While I hummed taps, Cody pulled the lever.

Later on, when we knelt by his bed to whisper good-night prayers, Cody came up with this eulogy:

"God, my fish died . . . he's gone to heaven . . . Heaven for a fish is the toilet."

That's when I broke up. I laughed about it the rest of the evening.

Birds and fish supply good lessons—and sometimes a few laughs. But when it's a human in the casket, it's no laughing matter.

We must all face three inescapable human dilemmas—living as an enemy of God, suffering as a slave of sin, and fearing the sting of death. But they aren't without solutions.

Too Little, Too Late

The world system has a catalog of man-made remedies. Some are out on a shaky limb, some sound credible:

- Beverly Hills gurus and New Age prophets tell us to surround our lives with crystals and meditate.

- Reformers pronounce that the human malady can be corrected through stiffer laws, gun control, and education.

- The enlightened suggest accountability, small groups, family nights, and religious instruction.

Some of these have merit. But none can counter the effects of man's three big struggles. That's because their common denominator involves things you must *do*.

For instance, man's sin nature creates despair. Despair causes him to turn to drugs. The drugs jeopardize his life and guarantee him an earlier trip to the cemetery. The world responds with a *program* . . . "Just say no!" But you can't say "no" until you've first said "yes" to something that gives meaning to your existence. That's where faith comes in. The only solution to the three dilemmas is faith. Not faith in general, but faith in particular.

An Answer to My Three Biggest Problems

Man's tragedy became God's cause—and a divine Rescue Mission was designed to eradicate the problem. Knowing the human nightmare better than man himself, God offered the only solution.

The solution was His own Son, nailed to a Roman cross on a hill in Palestine. The Lord Jesus Christ hung between heaven and earth and created the only bridge between man and God.

God saw fit to allow His Son to die as a substitute for man. Man-made sins were paid for through a God-made plan.

Instead of making the solution something *we do*, God has made it something *He has done*.

Answer to Problem #1: My position is changed

Jesus has given me a new position with the Father. Instead of God's enemy, I am His dearly loved, adopted child.

Answer to Problem #2: My sin problem is solved

I am no longer a slave to sin. God has transformed me from the inside out. He changes my longings and desires. He provides the only true power over sin because He first paid the price for its penalty.

Answer to Problem #3: My eternal life is assured

As a result of embracing Christ's work on the cross by faith, I have the assurance of eternal life. Death becomes a comma, a transition between time and eternity. It is a de-clawed, toothless tiger that makes a lot of noise but presents no lasting threat.

Hearts Set Free

Faith is the foundation of our legacy. It enables us to

give one of the most significant gifts of all to our children. It prepares them to die.

Death is inescapable. There are no exceptions. So why not relieve our children of the burden? Living is a lot easier when we don't have to keep looking over our shoulder.

Once we are prepared to die, we are free to live!

There's a verse to that effect just left of center in your Bible. In the nineteenth chapter of Job are the words of a man who stared death in the eye and refused to be intimidated. Listen to the confidence of this righteous man:

> I know that my Redeemer lives, and that in the end he will stand upon the earth. And after my skin has been destroyed, yet in my flesh I will see God; I myself will see him with my own eyes—I, and not another (vv. 25-27, NIV).

Now that's confidence!

It's that same confidence that our children can enjoy at an early age.

Good Intentions—Bad Assumptions

I've been working with kids for almost two decades. No one debates me about the critical need for a dynamic faith in a child's life. Yet sadly, I've observed that one of the biggest obstacles to that goal are well-intentioned parents with a bad set of assumptions.

What I'm about to discuss is a touchy subject. You need to read carefully.

Parents want the assurance that their children are safe and secure in an eternal relationship with God. They know the Bible makes it clear that no accountable adults will ever see heaven unless they have first given their hearts to Christ through faith.

Naturally, they want to remove any roadblocks to faith. So they cloister their children during the early years. They pick their friends, monitor the information coming into them, and try to counter any false notions about life.

So far so good.

They also assume that the best defense against the powers of darkness is a good offense with the Power of Light. Church, Sunday school, parochial schools, and Bible clubs become a regular part of their children's lives.

Once again, they're on the right track.

But two things parents do with their children's belief system can backfire—blowing up a young spirit in the process.

One mistake is to assume that training *about* the Christian life is going to guarantee the assumed result—that a child will embrace this knowledge and take it to heart.

But Christianity is not a head trip. It is a modeled belief system supported by knowledge. A child will not accept a life plan to which his parents only give mental assent. If a child is going to accept your faith as his own, *he must see it lived out.* Alive and breathing and functioning. In you!

I can't count the times I've witnessed the tears of a mother lamenting her wayward child. Oddly, all of those laments seem to share a common theme . . .

". . . He went to Sunday school and church every week of his life. How could he end up in jail?"

". . . we spent all of that money on her Christian school education, and what did it get us? A grandson and an unwed daughter."

But in many of these cases, I know that at least one of the parents isn't walking the talk. Compromise has been a habit for the dad or mom, and that's all it takes to alienate the child from the parent's belief system.

None of us is perfect. Every parent makes mistakes. But there is an observable difference between a dad who acknowledges faith and a dad who *lives* by it . . . between a mom whose belief is a compartment of her life and a mom whose belief envelops her life.

Parents must be prepared to lay their faith on life's firing line. It needs to be visible, embraceable, measurable, and transferable.

I have said there are two ways well-intentioned parents can create obstacles in the path of their children's faith. If the first issue was touchy, the next one is a mine field.

Good Intentions—Bad Timing

Good Christian parents concern themselves with their young children's need for salvation. Sometimes that takes the form of words like these:

"Each person needs to invite Jesus into his heart if he wants to be forgiven of his sins and have the opportunity to go to heaven. We love Jesus, and have asked Him into our hearts. Wouldn't you like to do the same?"

There is nothing incorrect or insincere about that statement. The parent who tenderly speaks these words to his or her child only has the best interest of the child at heart. But if we can step back and examine the situation for a moment, we may become aware of some dangers.

Children want eternal life. They want to respond to God. But even more, they want to *please* their parents.

Young, impressionable children will embrace almost anything their parents say. Unfortunately, the faith many of them exercise is not faith in Christ, *but faith in their parents.* Faith in their parents is great, but it cannot do anything to rectify their hostility toward God, their problem with sin, and their appointment with death.

Children who embrace their parents' faith rather than forming their own can develop a false sense of security. When these children hit the independent years of adolescence and start to lean away from the values of Mom and Dad, a quiet void or an open hostility toward spiritual ideas may develop.

Parents can avoid this trap by creating a loving, caring, spiritual environment, fleshed out in a disciplined way in the home. The gospel message transmitted through church, school, and family conversations can be used by the Holy Spirit to draw the child to Himself . . . on *His* timetable.

Darcy and I discussed this at length before we had any children. We made a decision to live out the gospel to the best of our ability, acknowledge our daily dependence on Christ, but avoid overt appeals to our children to respond to Christ. We pray for them, and with them. At this writing we have two children that are quite young. They love church and the teachings of Christ. But we resist the temptation to push for a commitment or decision. We continue to wait and pray for the Sovereign God to draw them to Himself.

Our oldest daughter Karis chose to give her life to the Lord as a result of hearing the gospel through someone else. She quizzed the person for over an hour, and on her own initiated the idea to come to the Lord. We could see the contrast in her life the next day. Our gift to her will be the commitment to maintain a loving, Christian environment in which her faith can grow.

The Faith Journey

The week between Christmas and New Year's Day, Karis traveled with me to the Poconos of Pennsylvania. I was speaking at a holiday getaway for several hundred high school students. The schedule called for me to address the kids each morning and evening. That left my afternoons free to enjoy the company of my daughter.

The retreat center sat on the banks of the Delaware River. Each afternoon we took off in the camp mini-van to explore the villages and towns that dotted the countryside of Eastern Pennsylvania.

One particular afternoon lingers in my mind. The scene couldn't have been more picturesque. The mood couldn't have been more satisfying. Karis and I had visited several antique stores, enjoyed a soda at a restored ice cream parlor, taken a walk across a footbridge, and studied the epitaphs in a nineteenth-century cemetery.

On the way back to camp, I was driving parallel to the river through a tunnel of trees. The leftover autumn leaves whipped up behind us as we rode along in silence.

I was contented with my world.

Karis broke the silence.

"Daddy, what if it's not true?"

I looked at her. "What if what's not true, honey?"

"What if all the stuff about Jesus and the Bible isn't true?"

Everything inside me shifted to the alarm mode. The quiet mood of father-daughter fellowship vanished. The afternoon suddenly turned cold. I was witnessing one of the first true tests of my first-born's faith.

All my instincts pushed me to race back to the camp, grab my Bible, and start going over the fundamentals of inspiration and the deity of Christ. But something inside made me feel that this wasn't the time or the place. A little girl was asking an honest question. She needed a response . . . not a reaction.

I pulled the van over to the side of the road and sat quietly for a moment, breathing a quick prayer, trying to determine the best way to approach her question.

She decided to elaborate.

"What I mean is . . . well, I was wondering how we can know for certain if all of the stories about the Bible are true. But I've been worried that doubting is wrong."

"No Karis, doubting isn't wrong. It's human. I've had doubts before. That's why it all comes down to faith. God gives us enough evidence and enough information to make an educated decision. But He doesn't fill in all of the blanks. He leaves just enough room for us to have to make a choice to trust. I'm not concerned that you might occasionally doubt. I'll only be concerned if you let your doubts run your life."

At that moment Karis recalled a verse she had learned somewhere along the way. "Without faith," she quoted, "it is impossible to please God."

I was glad I, too, had memorized that verse, because I could finish it for her. ". . . for he who comes to God must believe that He is, and that He is a rewarder of those who seek Him."

The life of faith isn't a done deal just because our kids prayed a prayer one day. It's a walk. A journey. And our job of modeling it is never over. As we live it out each day, we find that we, too, benefit from the promise.

"He is a rewarder of those who seek Him."

TEN WAYS TO TEACH YOUR CHILDREN FAITH

1. Let them find you reading your Bible every morning when they arise.

2. Have them pray at meals and at bedtime.

3. Watch the old movie *Inherit the Wind* with them, then discuss their feelings.

4. Trace the root of faith in their family tree. If you are a first generation believer, tell them your testimony.

5. Plant a garden and explain how you have to exercise patience and trust in God's laws of nature.

6. Have them prepare a three-minute testimony about their faith in God.

7. Have them share their testimony with a friend.

8. Remind them of answered prayer.

9. Pray for an unsaved or sick friend or relative every day.

10. Using qualified professionals, take your older children through a course that emphasizes faith in a rope, learning such techniques as rock-climbing or rappelling down a cliff. This should provide many word pictures to discuss topics like faith, trust, and responding to crisis.

Bonus: In the spring, plan an October trip to Wrigley Field. (Now, *that's* faith.)

CHAPTER FIVE

Integrity

Life isn't easy when you're overshadowed by a sibling. And when that sibling happens to be Michael Jackson—the moonwalking, sequined-gloved singer, dancer, and drinker of Pepsi—life can seem downright impossible.

Jackson is a member of a large and extremely talented family. With several brothers and a couple of sisters, the Jacksons have entertained the world for almost three decades. Michael has sat on the throne of the rock and roll industry almost since Elvis died, and it doesn't look as if he's planning on relinquishing his crown any time soon.

He has a sister two years his elder named La Toya. La Toya has cut a few albums and made a few videos, but she's never received the recognition that the rest of her brothers and sisters have.

Until just recently.

When you get desperate, you're capable of doing almost anything. I sense from an article in *USA Today* that La Toya got fed up with life in the shadows.

She bared her soul in the "Nation's Newspaper" . . . and then bared everything else in a *Playboy* "pictorial essay."

"Why did you do it?" the newspaper wanted to know. The interviewer sounded out the reactions of her "protective" parents and her famous brother, and then went straight to the heart of the matter. I found La Toya's answers telling. Let me quote directly from the article.

> "I look at the human body as a work of art. I don't think there's anything to be ashamed of," Jackson says. "In America, we've been covered for so many years. If we bare something, it's a disgrace. But it really isn't."
>
> In fact, she was in Spain last July when *Playboy* first approached her. "I first said, 'Absolutely not. *I'm not that kind of girl.*'"
>
> When the magazine *offered more money*, she and Gordon (her agent) investigated. "Then I realized *there's absolutely nothing wrong with this*, not to mention that many of the women in Spain were walking around topless."[4]

I added the italics to emphasize her words, but I didn't tamper with the text. That's the order the paragraphs appeared in *USA Today*. They pronounce a verdict on her character.

Integrity is what we are when we are hidden from the gaze of others. It's forged in the back rooms of our private lives. Eventually, however, the truth comes out in the open.

I felt sorry for La Toya. I know she's an adult and responsible for her actions. But I couldn't help but think that the one-dimensional life of a limelight family left some gaps in her character. In the end, her own words placed the noose around her reputation.

An Uphill Marathon

When I think of a legacy of love, I picture parents who carefully develop a child's integrity. All other skills and talents, regardless of how carefully defined, must submit to the demands of integrity.

That's because integrity protects us. We never have to keep the lies straight or catalog the deceptions. There's never a worry about what we said or what we did. Integrity shines out of our life like an inner light, and people find it easy to place their trust in us.

King Solomon had a lot to say about integrity. He often contrasted one truth with another so that each idea punched home the relevancy of the other. If you break open your Bible to the tenth chapter of his collection of proverbs, you'll see quite a gem gleaming in verse 9. Listen to his wisdom.

He who walks in integrity walks securely, but he who perverts his ways will be found out.

They ought to carve that into the halls of Congress and hang it by the teleprompter facing every television evangelist. Every dad and mom could profit by it, too.

When I shipped off to seminary, meandered through the ivory towers of theology, and finally graduated into ministry, I was naive about a lot of things. For one, I had no idea how intensely I would be scrutinized.

It didn't take long before I realized that the people to whom I ministered held up a different yardstick to their own character than the one they held up to mine. That's because the ministry is a character profession. It's one of those livelihoods that demands consistency. You can be an excellent plumber even though you cheat on your wife. You can be a sought-after attorney even though you are addicted to pornography. But try to juggle those vices while standing behind the pulpit and you will soon find yourself looking for a new platform.

Well, guess what?

Parenting is a character profession!

The children who sleep in our back bedrooms, inhale the food out of our refrigerators, and hog our telephones don't grade our lives on a curve. When they see us mess up, you can be sure they'll mark it down on their parental scorecard. That's why we must try especially hard to model exemplary character.

Sure, all of us let them down somewhere along the way. We parents have a bad habit of being human. But our human frailties can never excuse us from daily monitoring our standards of integrity.

The good news is that love covers a multitude of mistakes. The bad news is that if the mistakes are consistent and glaring enough, our children will question our love.

Therefore, *we* must embrace integrity before we can transfer it to our children. It's a twenty-four-hour-a-day, seven-days-a-week, fifty-two-weeks-a-year assignment. And a long-term job like that naturally breeds fatigue and frustration. My wife and I get tired of always having to be in a teaching mode. We get frustrated with the kids when we think they have mastered something, only to have them turn around the next minute and act like they've never heard of the concept before.

It gives me an idea of how God must feel with us.

Integrity is an uphill marathon, not a sprint. It's not something "once taught, forever caught." You can be sure that when serious integrity problems appear in a person's life, they result from a slow leak, not a blowout.

On the other hand, a life of consistent, righteous living not only results in a proven track record of integrity, but becomes an eternal investment in our families. The truth is that integrity, like any habit, gets easier with practice.

That's what Solomon said. Look at his words in Proverbs 20:7:

A righteous man who walks in his integrity—how blessed are his sons after him.

Children led through life by a mother and father of integrity have it much easier when they become adults. Ethics aren't debatable. Truth isn't confused. It's easier for them to maintain a consistent walk because that's been their consistent example throughout childhood.

I'm struck by the use of the word "walk" when the writers of Scripture refer to integrity. The process of building integrity is much like developing a walk of faith. It assumes effort, it requires dependency on God, and it's never over.

David, the shepherd/poet, used the idea of walking to describe a life of integrity. He stated it as plainly as a person can in Psalm 101. Look at verses 2 and 3:

I will give heed to the blameless way . . . I will walk within my house in the integrity of my heart.
I will set no worthless thing before my eyes.

Unfortunately, David didn't always review his own poems. One night, years after he became king, he was walking in his rooftop patio and looked out over his city. Below him in the open air bathed Bathsheba, another man's wife. Not only did he disregard his own advice in Psalm 101, but he fixed a lustful gaze on her. It was all downhill after that.

A careful inspection of his life shows that his sense of integrity had been eroding for years. He had been shirking his responsibilities and taking life easy. Second Samuel 11:1 (NIV) says it clearly: "In the spring, at the time when kings go off to war, *David sent Joab out* . . . But *David remained in Jerusalem.*"

His integrity didn't vanish with a **Bang!**, but a *Sssssssss*.

Knowing What We're Dealing With

If we want to avoid David's plight in his older years, we need to embrace the truth he taught in his hungry years. To walk in our homes in the integrity of our hearts assumes we know what integrity demands. A standard dictionary can shed a lot of light on this.

Integrity has a Latin heritage. It comes from the word *integer*. You've heard that word before. Back in elementary school we all were introduced to the term in basic math. Just in case you've forgotten, an integer is a whole number, like 5, 28, or 162. Its counterpart is a fraction. Integrity is defined as "an unimpaired condition, the quality or state of being complete or undivided."

When Jesus sat on the side of a mountain teaching the people, he discussed integrity. He said, "No one can serve two masters; for either he will hate the one and love the other, or he will hold to one and despise the other. You cannot serve God and mammon" (Matthew 6:24).

The secret to knowing what's expected of a person of integrity is wrapped up in that statement "you cannot serve God and mammon." Integrity is serving God. The easiest way to serve God is to live by His standards.

Integrity can be broken into three parts: Truth, Convictions, and Reputation. Teaching our children how to be men and women of integrity assumes that we know what these three things are, and that we have a plan to transfer them.

Truth

I don't sit around reading the *Guinness Book of World Records*. But I am impressed with some of the people whose abilities are outlined in its pages. To me, there's one name that deserves to stand above the rest. Although this woman's name is in the book more for who she is than for what she's done, she nonetheless gets a lot of my respect. Her name is Marilyn Vos Savant, and *Guinness* claims she has the highest measured IQ in the world.

I like the answer Ms. Savant once gave to a pregnant question about the might of ideas. "What is the most powerful concept and what makes it powerful?" the interviewer asked. Came the simple but profound answer: "What is the most powerful concept? *Truth*. What makes it so powerful? It is so powerful because whether we like it or not, there isn't a darn thing we can do about it."[5]

Facts don't change because we ignore them. We can deny gravity, but it won't change its pull on us if we decide to do a one-and-a-half off a roof.

Children need to be raised in an environment of truth. Guile, dishonesty, and deception must be recognized as enemies of the family and enemies to its future. Integrity protects us. Truth sets us free (John 8:32). Conscientious parents must devote themselves to high standards of truth.

It naturally starts with parents. Children will always have a difficult time rising above the high water mark set by Mom and Dad.

A sad example of this snuck up on me one day as I rode with a friend through a neighborhood. He owned a few rental properties and mentioned that he needed to stop by one of them to pick up a check. I didn't mind the detour, so we stopped at a little bungalow and rapped on the door. I quickly became impressed with the charm, intelligence, and closeness of the family who lived within.

After a few minutes my friend brought up a subject they had apparently discussed before. The family had been interested in buying his house, so my friend had researched the property and decided on a price he felt was fair. They stopped him mid-sentence to announce that they had considered it but wouldn't be able to make the purchase. They proudly told us that the bulk of their income came to them "under the table." They had saved thousands of dollars in taxes, but because of the low income claimed on their tax returns, they could not qualify for the necessary loans.

I was instantly turned off by this family's deception and fraud. It bothered me that these folks could so proudly boast about their dishonesty right in front of their kids.

A week later my friend visited them again. I wasn't with him this time, but he told me what happened. Just as he was about to knock on the door he heard shouts coming from inside. The parents were screaming at their son and he was firing back at them. My friend decided to come back another time, but hesitated long enough to hear the reason for the conflict. The boy had been expelled from school because he had been caught cheating . . . again.

There are no shortcuts with truth. When people think that they can compromise their way to wealth, position, or influence, the answer from above is, "You can't get there from here."

A legacy of love insists that we relentlessly monitor and scrutinize both our lives and those of our children. At some time and in some way, every child will test how serious we are about our standards of truth. That's when we must be prepared to take our stand.

But children don't always test the boundaries when we're around. They are notorious for waiting until we are out of the picture so that they can push the limits on the second string—babysitters.

Let me slip back to the Kimmel archives to relate a story. By the way, I asked my daughter to see if it was okay to mention this. Everything is cleared with her.

Darcy and I had an appointment one morning and needed to be away from the house during breakfast. We arranged for a babysitter to watch the kids and see that Karis got off to school.

Karis was in first grade and was allowed to pick out her school clothes one day a week. At that age, that's about all a parent can endure. First graders have unusual tastes in clothes. With that in mind Darcy made the selection four days a week. As Karis got older the responsibility would be handed over to her completely, and by fifth grade she'll be making the choice every day. But this particular day, Darcy had set out the clothes our daughter was to wear.

When the babysitter awakened Karis, she noticed the outfit. But when she came back a few minutes later to check on progress, she noticed Karis putting on a different set of clothes. She peeked in the closet and saw that the outfit chosen by Darcy had been hung back on the bar. Karis had not been careful to wedge it in properly and it was still sticking out.

The babysitter asked Karis if the outfit she was putting on was the one her mother intended her to wear. "Yes," she said.

Lie number one.

Was she sure about that? "Yes," she said again.

Lie number two.

The babysitter left Karis's room and went out to the kitchen to think. Soon she decided that she couldn't let Karis get away with it. She marched back in, lifted Karis's face so their eyes were inches apart, and asked her again.

"Karis. Look me in the eyes and answer my question. Is the outfit that you're putting on the one your mother intended you to wear?"

"No." (That's better!)

"Where is the outfit that she intended you to wear?"

"I stuck it back in the closet."

"Well, change clothes, and while you're doing it I'll tell you what I think about lying."

For the next few minutes Karis got an earful on the subject of deception and dishonesty. She got some chores to do as punishment and was told her parents would get a full report.

That evening I was in our bedroom changing my shoes when Karis walked by my door. I called her in, sat her on my lap, and asked her to tell me about getting ready for school.

She dropped her head and told me that she had switched the outfit Mom had picked out. I asked her if that was all. She went on to confess that she had lied to the babysitter.

"Karis," I said, "you didn't get up early enough to switch the outfit before the babysitter saw it. You didn't even do a good job of putting the outfit back on the bar inside your closet."

Then I looked her in the eye and said, "Karis, you aren't a very good liar. And I'm going to do everything I can to keep you that way."

Karis's crime wasn't all that big. But I've noticed that little crimes can easily become dress rehearsals for big ones. That's why we've got to deal with them all.

And that's a big part of leaving a legacy of love. We have to be involved in our children's lives enough to monitor the fine points of their behavior. And when we aren't there, we have to make sure that others are standing in the gap. If we commit to keeping our children lousy at sin, while at the same time setting the boundaries for truth, they are more likely to choose the high road of integrity.

Convictions

You don't have to walk too far from the cobblestone streets of downtown Annapolis, Maryland, before you happen upon a three-story brick building that once was the home of the "Fighting Panthers." That was the mascot that the founders of my high school picked out around the turn of the century. This is where I spent my high school years trying to get an education during the last half of the 1960s.

In the middle of this giant building, just inside the main front doors, was the auditorium where we held our assemblies, performed our plays, and listened to our concerts. It was to this auditorium we were summoned to learn of problems facing our country.

The average student of the sixties was preoccupied with political corruption, racial unrest, and the Vietnam War. Because of the size of our school and its proximity to Washington, D.C., we had more than our share of activist students. Several times during high school I had to sit in the auditorium and listen to caustic debates as students fought faculty, who fought students, who fought each other.

A few summers ago I was back in Annapolis and took my two oldest children to see my school. They were as unimpressed with it as I had been. But in the years since, my mind had repainted this old building in softer shades of understanding. I wasn't there two minutes before I was wading through nostalgia.

The building had long since been condemned as unfit for students and had been turned into an art studio. But the auditorium was just like it had been when I was a student. And there, engraved in foot-high letters on the wall above the stage, was a quote—a bit of wisdom that went largely unnoticed by my classmates.

This time I read the quote with the understanding of an adult who had a few years of experience under his belt. The words had an entirely different effect on me than they did during the churning decade of the sixties. The quote read:

THE MEASURE OF A MAN
IS THE DEPTH OF HIS CONVICTIONS
THE BREADTH OF HIS INTERESTS
AND THE HEIGHT OF HIS IDEALS

Perhaps the reason we had paid so little attention to the statement was that we had lost confidence in the leadership of our country. Another reason could be that we were selfish, naive high school students who wouldn't have noticed it regardless of who led us.

I think our principal would have voted for the second option. Regardless, there is a cause-and-effect relationship between the standards of those who lead us and the convictions that we ultimately embrace.

In the last chapter I said that parents must prepare their children for death. Once they are prepared to die, they are free to live.

But convictions add a second variable to this equation. Faith prepares us to die, but convictions give us something worth dying for. They are essential to a legacy of love because . . .

. . . *once we have something worth dying for, then we have something worth **living** for.*

While our children are still children we must instill those bedrock convictions that will offer them a firm place to stand. Only that which is timeless can withstand the ravages of time.

Faith, Family, and Freedom are three convictions for which I'd lay everything on the line. Building such convictions into our children gives them an insurance policy for their future. They are civilization's bottom line.

Convictions are a step beyond principles. Many people live according to a few pithy sayings. The principled life is a mottoed life. It's a plaque-on-the-wall and verse-in-my-purse mindset that can be abandoned as easily as it can be embraced.

When I move my reason for living from catch phrases to fighting words, I step outside my world of comfort and must be ready to risk everything for the things I hold dear.

Convictions based on the absolute truths of Scripture prepare a child to grow into an adult unafraid of the issues that seek to undermine his faith. Those same convictions provide an unerring rule for encouraging and protecting the people he loves.

Reputation

Truth is at the core of integrity. Convictions enable truth to take action in our life. Reputation is the outcome of living by convictions.

It's just at this point where our children need to understand that the reputation we gain by acknowledging truth and living by convictions may not bring us popularity.

William Wilberforce, the famed English parliamentarian, fought for forty-five years to abolish slave trade and emancipate the slaves. He committed his entire professional life to this cause. He endured the ridicule, hostility, and threats of those who capitalized on the capture and marketing of humans. Had he not understood truth, had he not embraced convictions, he could never have gone the distance. His commitment to the sanctity of human life grew out of his relationship with the God who gives life.

If we're not careful, we could confuse popularity with reputation. There's something intoxicating about the praise of men. Do not be misled: If our aim becomes winning the praise and approval of the public, our convictions will eventually be compromised.

Jesus said, "Blessed are you when men cast insults at you, and persecute you, and say all kinds of evil against you falsely, on account of Me. Rejoice, and be glad, for your reward in heaven is great" (Matthew 5:11-12).

Leaving a legacy of love means that I will teach my children to draw their approval and sense of reputation from God. As Paul said, "If God is for us, who can be against us?" (Romans 8:31, NIV). When we fully appreciate our relationship with Christ, we won't need the praise of man. David summed up this very point in the first verse of his most famous psalm. He said, "The LORD is my shepherd, I shall not want." In other words, "Because the Lord is my Shepherd, what more could I possibly need?"

Our children get opportunities to put theory into practice early on.

• When locker room jokes make a mockery of decency

• When the school gigolo boasts of the notches in his dashboard

• When the class gossip turns her caustic tongue on our child

• When the boss encourages the bending of ethics in order to increase the bottom line.

Truth, convictions, and a godly reputation will continue to stand long after the rest of the world has caved in. Loving parents need to commit themselves to building integrity into each of their children's lives.

The Demands of Leadership

By now you may be wondering how to pull this off. Let me introduce an adjective that I think best describes the kind of parent that can build integrity into a child's life. Here it is: *sophisticated*.

That may take a little explanation. That word for many people means stuffy, detached, superior. But let's allow Webster to do the talking for a second. He defines sophisticated as "complex," "worldly-wise," "finely experienced and aware." To be that kind of a parent does not require a high IQ. It does require a lot of commitment.

There's a great example of a sophisticated father in Proverbs 1-9. This dad has a keen sense of the street without allowing himself to be contaminated. He understands the laws of consequence and reward. He teaches his son to avoid the traps of pride, money, and sex.

This father does not teach his son in abstract, theological cliches. He saves the boy a trip to the wrong side of town by warning him in honest, loving terms about the wages of sin. One thing that makes this sophisticated father so helpful is that he consistently shows how many of the benefits of eternal life can be enjoyed in the present.

In other words, the truth that we believe, the convictions that we stand for, and the godly reputation that we gain allow us to enjoy the privilege and reward of our eternal position with the Lord *right now.* We don't have to check out to check in.

Integrity is one of those subjects that can't be exhausted in a chapter. Whole libraries couldn't exhaust the topic. That's the nature of anything that's worth our life.

Our children are worth our life, too. They are worth the frustration and sweat that it takes to imprint them with this essential trait called integrity.

Let me sign off this chapter with a poem that struck me as a young, impressionable boy. It's wise counsel from Rudyard Kipling's pen and sums up this great attribute known as integrity.

"IF"

If you can keep your head when all about you
    Are losing theirs and blaming it on you,
If you can trust yourself when all men doubt you,
    But make allowance for their doubting too;
If you can wait and not be tired by waiting,
    Or being lied about, don't deal in lies,
Or being hated don't give way to hating,
    And yet don't look too good, nor talk too wise;

If you can dream—and not make dreams your master;
    If you can think—and not make thought your aim;
If you can meet with Triumph and Disaster
    And treat those two impostors just the same;
If you can bear to hear the truth you've spoken
    Twisted by knaves to make a trap for fools,
Or watch the things you gave your life to, broken,
    And stoop and build 'em up with worn-out tools;

If you can make one heap of all your winnings
    And risk it on one turn of pitch-and-toss,
And lose, and start again at your beginnings,
    And never breathe a word about your loss;
If you can force your heart and nerve and sinew
    To serve your turn long after they are gone,
And so hold on when there is nothing in you
    Except the Will which says to them: "Hold On!"

If you can talk with crowds and keep your virtue,
    Or walk with Kings—nor lose the common touch,
If neither foes nor loving friends can hurt you,
    If all men count with you, but none too much;
If you can fill the unforgiving minute
    With sixty seconds' worth of distance run,
Yours is the Earth and everything that's in it,
    And—which is more—you'll be a Man, my son![6]

TEN WAYS TO TEACH YOUR CHILDREN INTEGRITY

1. Drive the speed limit.

2. Never ask your children to lie for you.

3. Apologize when you wrong your children.

4. Send them into a store with more money than they need to buy a particular item. When they come out, see if they offer the change. Deal with them accordingly.

5. Never tolerate even the smallest lie.

6. Pick someone out of the newspaper who committed a crime, and ask the kids' opinion about it.

7. Fathers, never allow your sons to be disrespectful or rude to their mother.

8. Set up tasks that require their follow-through without supervision, and see if they carry out instructions on their own.

9. Take your children to visit their ancestors' graves. If you know any anecdotes about these ancestors (whether positive or negative), take time to share a few stories.

10. Have them memorize twenty verses on integrity. (You might want to start with the Ten Commandments.)

CHAPTER SIX

Poise

Life is unpredictable. We need to be prepared for anything.

Like the time my foot was a little heavier on the gas pedal than the sign on the side of the road permitted. The sign, of course, was inanimate and unable to care whether I obeyed or not. It was another story with the policeman parked just out of sight. He wasn't inanimate, and *did* seem to care. He cared enough to fill my rear view mirror with flashing blue lights.

Actually, I care very much about traffic regulations and do my best to adhere to them. But at this particular moment, on this particular night, my mind was elsewhere. It was in a nursery at a local hospital where I had an infant daughter trying to decide whether to live or die.

Apparently I was doing fifty-two in a forty-mile-per-hour zone. But at that moment, suffering more from shock and numbness than raw panic, I didn't notice the speedometer. I had no idea what had gone wrong with my baby girl and no idea what was going to happen to her. Darcy's call from the hospital had awakened me in the middle of the night. She was weeping and told me that our newborn, Shiloh, had simply shut down. Everything just stopped. The doctors had got her going again but were extremely concerned.

So, right in the middle of my nightmare, one of Scottsdale's finest decided to give the bad dream an extra twist. When I saw his lights I immediately pulled into a grocery store parking lot. I got out and stood near the back of my car with my hands open and outside my jacket. His headlights were blinding, but I wanted to make sure he could easily see me.

The officer approached me. Fast.

He must have been having a bad night too, because as soon as I started to explain my dilemma he ordered me to shut my mouth, give him my license, and go stand by my car. When I tried to clarify that I had a bit of an emergency, he put his billy club under my chin, nudged my head up, and repeated his command:

"I told you to shut up, give me your licence, and go stand by your car."

As a boy, I had been taught to respect and obey authority. Throughout my years as a youth worker I have consistently passed this message on to the kids with whom I've worked. But at that moment, in that parking lot, looking into the face of that officer, everything inside of me wanted to unleash, attack, and destroy.

Fortunately, I had also been taught as a boy that a billy club and a .38 beat a full grown, unarmed man every time. I knew that I wanted to get to Scottsdale Memorial

Hospital. But I wanted to walk into the maternity ward rather than being wheeled into the emergency room.

So I shut up, handed him my license, and leaned against the back door of our family wagon.

The officer popped into his car to report the appropriate information and then came back to me. He asked for the paperwork on my car. I got it out and handed it to him. I was no longer concerned about explaining my plight. I did mention that he was not dealing properly with me, but he ignored me.

I leaned against my car for fifteen minutes while he took his time writing out my ticket. I seethed for the first ten minutes. Ultimately, I was forced to hand my anger to God and ask Him to take it away. My anger would be of no value to my wife and daughter. I resigned myself to the ticket and to getting out of the situation with minimal hassles.

The officer was polite and professional when he brought me the ticket to sign. He called me "Mr. Kimmel," gave me my court date, and volunteered that I ought to appear before the judge for a decision.

After I signed the ticket he looked me in the eyes. "I suggest that you slow down, Mr. Kimmel. Your little girl has enough problems without having to be an orphan, too."

So he did hear me! I couldn't believe it. Up to this point, I figured he couldn't care less about me or my family. Maybe there *was* a heart inside that uniform.

I've come to understand that behind every problem there is an unfulfilled need. I could focus on the unprofessionalism and rudeness of the officer, or I could assume there was something else causing his abrupt behavior. After all, my town doesn't let anyone put on a badge until he or she has been thoroughly trained.

A couple of weeks later I appeared for my court date. I sat among a motley collection of misdemeanors waiting for the judge to appear.

My case was the last one called. I had watched Her Honor, the judge, find every single defendant guilty. I assumed my outcome would be the same and had brought my checkbook just in case.

The officer went first, explaining everything exactly as it happened, including the fact that he had spoken harshly to me and didn't give me an opportunity to speak, even though I was distressed over an emergency. The judge asked for my perspective. I simply told her that I was trying to get to the hospital faster than I should have. Everything else was just as the officer had said. She asked how my daughter was doing. I gave her a progress report.

And then the judge gave me a good lesson on poise.

"Mr. Kimmel," she said, "the law is supposed to be blind. It's supposed to deal strictly with the facts and not show any partiality. However, justice must always be balanced by mercy. I think that you went through enough. I'm going to drop the violation . . . and the Court hopes that your daughter will be okay."

I walked out of the courtroom with the officer. When we got to the lobby I asked him why he had been so tough. That's when I learned that, just before pulling me over, he had suffered through an ordeal that had consumed most of his evening. He had pulled over a carload of teenagers, one of them had jumped him when he asked for a licence, and the rest fled. It took him several minutes of scuffling before he was able to handcuff his assailant. It took even longer to apprehend the ones who ran away. He was edgy and unusually defensive because of this earlier confrontation. (His unfulfilled need was a concern for his personal safety, even to the point of foregoing proper police procedure when pulling over a distressed citizen!)

Shifting Internal Gears

This incident can teach us several points about leaving a legacy of love. Sometime during our years of influence over our children we need to teach the fine art of shifting internal gears. Our kids have to develop *a keen sense of the appropriate*. That's poise. Children forced to move into their adult years without it will feel handicapped. One of the most loving gifts we can present our children is the ability to respond to life in a balanced way.

My parents had prepared me to face my crises with my daughter and with the policeman long before that terrible night rolled around. Their careful instruction about fear, anger, distress, conflict, and shock allowed me to face a dilemma decades later with minimal difficulty. When you think of what *could* have happened and what *did* . . . when you think of what I *could* have said but *chose not to* . . . it underlines the critical nature of poise.

For the record, I've had my share of poorly timed statements. A person who has as much to say as I do usually needs some great recipes for crow. Our best efforts with our children will not spare them future mistakes. What we want to do is develop their skills of poise well enough that those mistakes will be fewer.

Compassionate Parents

Instilling poise is a vital part of a legacy of love. It demonstrates our compassion for our children. The dictionary defines compassion as "sympathetic consciousness of others' distress together with a desire to alleviate it." We are being compassionate when we transfer to our children the skills needed to maintain a poised life. Compassion means anticipating their distresses in advance and doing something to minimize potential damage. A poised person has a more refined set of internal directions.

He or she is prepared in advance for shifts in circumstances or surroundings that could cause problems.

We can take this a step further. Poise not only helps us to minimize the bad, but to maximize the good. Parents leave a legacy of love to their children when they transfer skills that make the most of moments and relationships. The calm and confidence that my wife and I enjoy in our marriage is a direct result of the calm and confidence my parents modeled in their own relationship.

When poise is part of our mental checklist, we can be more tuned to opportunities that teach appropriate behavior as well as anticipate future problems.

Cody, my son, was about two years old when he first saw a piñata. We were at a Sunday school gathering when the host brought out a papier-mache donkey stuffed with candy. I explained to Cody about the candy inside, and that one of the blindfolded kids was going to whack it hard enough to break it open.

"The important thing," I told him, "is to be ready."

Sure enough, some husky kid hit a kink in the burro's cardboard armor and sent candy flying everywhere. Cody was the littlest kid in the group. Before he could even move, the older kids were all over the floor. They scarfed up every last piece of candy before Cody could grab one.

When he realized he was too late, he began to cry.

You pity your child in times like these. You want to go to one of the kids who seemed to have more than his share and bully some from him. You want to even the score.

But the piñata was a good illustration of life. Instead of trying to fight his battles for him (and be guilty of taking advantage of my size), I pulled him over to a corner of the yard where we could talk. We discussed defeat, disappointment, and how to face both of those realities in a proper way. Getting left out is part of life. Every once in a while we get chosen last—or not at all. But a poised person knows how to respond properly and move on. He knows everyone has to lose now and then.

About a year later Cody saw his second piñata. But this time he had two advantages. His first was that he had been in this situation before and knew what happens if you don't move quickly. But his second was better than the first—this time *he* was the biggest kid at the party. When the piñata burst, Cody dove like an eagle for a trout. Kids squealed and grabbed for a couple of seconds before every piece of candy had vanished.

Cody grabbed more than anyone else. He had stuffed his pockets and both fists full. We laughed. I congratulated him and let him enjoy the moment. But I couldn't let him move beyond this event without letting him see the situation from the other side. Jesus said that to whom much is given, much is required. I pulled Cody far enough away from the group so that he could see the expressions on the other kids' faces. That's when he noticed the tears.

Everybody gets a windfall once in a while, and God expects us to be sensitive to those whose fortunes don't match ours. I'm glad I didn't have to tell him to share. He parted with enough of his bounty to stop the tears of the kids who got left out.

A son or daughter's childhood years, though fleeting, offer many opportunities to teach appropriate responses to life's ups and downs.

Gentle Strength

Poise is gentle strength. It's a working knowledge of the two extremes of life and the ability to balance between them.

Life has a hard side and a soft side. Jesus' public ministry illustrated this every day. He knew the proper use of tears and laughter, muscle and reason, leadership and servanthood. He could sit in the dirt with lepers, get up, wash His hands and dine with royalty. He knew when it was time to stand and fight, and He knew the hour of surrender.

Jesus showed the most poise at His darkest hour. On the cross He maintained His concern for His mother, His compassion for the misguided crowd, His mercy for the repenting soul, and His respect for His Father.

No environment is more conducive to the teaching of poise than the home. A conscientious mom and dad are in the best position to observe, instruct, evaluate, and critique their children. Long after we are gone, our children can enjoy the benefits of our loving nurture as they move with confidence into their adult years.

The judge I mentioned at the beginning of this chapter understood the balancing act required of the law. There is a time for justice (hard), and there is a time for mercy (soft). The more we develop our ability to respond to the challenges of life, the more our children will be able to relax. (For more on this topic see the book, *Hard Side, Soft Side*, by Gary Smalley and Dr. John Trent, Focus on the Family Publishing.)

A Checklist for Poised Children

I'd like to suggest a checklist as I bring this chapter to a close. It's a tally of areas in a child's life where an appropriate, poised response could make all the difference.

In the Emotions

God has given His children two precious but fragile gifts. Cupped within our emotions, these gifts bubble up or spill out as needed. Their names are laughter and tears. Both are wonderful friends to the poised person. They can be enjoyed privately or given as an investment in others.

But like everything else in life, they can be abused, squandered, or employed at the wrong time. Tears can be manipulative. Laughter can be deceptive. Both can be shaped into destructive weapons.

Loving parents realize that it is important to train children on the proper use of laughter and tears. They must help their children make these dimensions of their emotions friends rather than enemies.

I've watched macho dads mislead their boys by telling them tears are for women and sissies. They aren't stopping the boys' tears with that kind of irresponsible advice, they're merely changing the direction that the tears are falling. Instead of falling from a boy's eyes, those little drops of emotion will splash on the floor of his soul—compressed, denied, and spoiled.

Tears are friends. Allies. Like the valve on top of a pressure cooker, they relieve the soul. Like laughter, they can soothe and medicate a broken heart. Denying their expression is cruel.

We parents can be equally guilty of wiping joy from our children's faces. Placing stoic expectations on souls that were tailor-made for laughter is a crime. A loving home needs to be bathed in laughter, with parents setting the pace.

Red Skelton said the reason he laughs so much is to keep from crying. Poised parents need to teach their children to walk that fine line that separates emotional extremes.

There are, of course, a thousand shades of feeling between tears and laughter. Emotional poise can enable children to move into their adult years prepared both to enjoy and invest a wide spectrum of emotion. Such children blessed with it received a wise and loving legacy.

In Social Settings

I can't think of a more obvious area for childhood development than the social skills. Yet I consistently run into adults who were virtually left on their own to develop social poise. The task is great, but we cannot call our parenting role complete if we neglect this vital area.

Regardless of our economic background, we need to equip our children to hobnob with hoboes and highbrows with equal ease. Whether they are having duck flambé with the homeless or flipping hamburgers on the hibachi with Princess Di, we need to pass on to them refinements that will allow them to move into any situation with confidence. The goal of this kind of training is not so that our children can impress people. Impressions can be as phony as the people we are impressing. The goal of refinements is to disarm, to put people at ease, and to allow moments to be maximized without awkward intrusions.

Poised people know how to listen, how to ask good questions, how to speak up when talking, how to look someone in the eye. They have a working knowledge of appropriate dress and manners, and they know how to prepare themselves to walk into strange environments without losing their sense of assurance. Tact is becoming a lost art, while rudeness is becoming a social trademark. Parents who want to equip their children to be poised socially need to coach them on the benefits of the former, and the liabilities of the latter.

Celebration does not come easily to people reared in conservative circles. In trying to avoid the excesses of a lost world, many evangelical Christians appear prideful or condescending. I seriously doubt that a few ballroom dancing lessons will turn our children into Solid Gold dancers, but a little such instruction may enable them to comfortably and graciously participate in the future wedding of a friend or relative. Sometimes it's the little things that make the biggest statements.

In Sexuality

Two words must be kept in mind as we bring our kids through the paces of life. They are *protection* and *preparation*.

In the early years, *protection* is by far the more important. We seek to monitor every aspect of our children's lives to make certain they are safe. As they get older, the priority naturally shifts to *preparation*. We must equip them to make wise choices when we aren't around to consult. Of all the dimensions of a child's life, the sexual dimension requires the most wise and prudent leadership that parents can muster. This area has the capacity to give more joy or to inflict more harm than any other part of the child's makeup.

Our strongest inclination is to protect. If I had my way, I wouldn't let my kids date until they're thirty-eight. But I'm not going to get my way. Nor will you. Like it or not, we live in a sex-saturated society. Our best attempts to shield our children from inappropriate sexual information will only work for the first couple of years.

Remember, I said, "If I had my way." My preferences are one thing, but reality is something else. I didn't establish the games that are being played in the world today, nor do I like the vile way that the powers of darkness are trying to contaminate the minds and hearts of our children. To conscientiously steward the next generation, we need to establish a strategy that can expose the true nature of sexual traps and counter the sexual momentum that our children will encounter every day.

If the best defense is a good offense, then one of the strongest ways to protect our children sexually is to prepare them to understand and properly respond to the sexual information that surrounds them.

It wasn't long after Darcy volunteered in Karis's kindergarten class that we realized it would be impossible to keep our little girl from being exposed to information about sex. Several of her classmates came from unsupervised homes. Uncensored movie channels and libraries of explicit videotapes were standard afternoon fare for some of these children. We realized that if she didn't hear the straight facts from us soon, she was going to hear a distorted and corrupted version from her classmates.

We chose to tell her the night before Darcy went to the hospital to have Shiloh (one of the convenient things about c-section deliveries is that you can schedule them). Earlier that day we had told her we were going to let her stay up past her normal bedtime in order to tell her something special. She sat next to her mother on the couch, but Darcy wanted me to do most of the explaining.

We didn't go into graphic detail, nor did we get highly technical, but before we were done Karis knew how babies were conceived. We also explained to her that like every beautiful thing God has created, man has figured out ways to pervert and destroy it. As she got older we would prepare her to recognize the perversion and protect herself from the traps the world system would set for her.

The last thing I told her was that she was not to go to school and tell all of her friends about this. That was their parents' responsibility—not hers.

When Darcy tucked her in that night, Karis thanked her for trusting her with the beautiful story of how babies are conceived.

End of story?

Well, not quite.

It's only fair to add a footnote. That April, four months after the Big Conversation, I got a call at my office. It was Darcy—she had just received a call from Karis's kindergarten teacher. It seems that it had been "show and tell" day, and one boy had brought a bowl full of baby guppies. He had held them up to the class and explained that the mother guppy lays the eggs in the water, and the father guppy swims through them—and that's how baby fish are made.

But then he made a mistake. If he would have stopped there, everything would have been fine. But once he made his next statement, there was no turning back. He said, "By the way, that's how people are made, too."

Karis said, "No, it's not."

He replied, "Oh, really? Then how *are* they made?"

So she stood up and told the class. Everything.

I figured that I was going to have to stay after school for a month, but it actually turned out all right. The teacher had called to relay the story for a reason. She said that Karis had the facts exactly right. She transferred them with ease. Furthermore, the teacher felt we had been right to tell her. (But I still wish that kid wouldn't have brought those fish to school.)

My wife and I have no guarantees that our children will make it to their wedding night sexually unscathed. But if they are poised enough to know how to appropriately respond to the world, we may just increase their odds.

The three areas I've discussed are merely a sampling. Poised and balanced children need careful leadership in every nuance of their lives. It takes sophisticated parents, like the Proverbs 1-9 father, to nurture them properly.

I'm thankful we have help. We have a sophisticated God. He's complex, but He's not complicated. He's omniscient, yet He has packaged His truth in relevant and understandable words. With this sophisticated God in our hearts and His sophisticated love in our families, we can be the kind of parents that give their children the gift of poise. Armed with a keen sense of the appropriate, those children will be ready for whatever tomorrow delivers to their door.

Some people call that common sense. I call it a legacy of love.

TEN WAYS TO TEACH YOUR CHILDREN POISE

1. Teach your children how to fight fair (check out Ephesians 4:25-32 for guidelines).

2. Invite a foreign student to your home and have your children prepare questions in advance to ask him or her.

3. Have your children write thank-you notes to people who regularly help them (teacher, friend, Sunday school teacher, pastor, etc.).

4. The next time you experience one of "Life's Most Embarrassing Moments," use it as an opportunity to tell your kids how you felt and what you did.

5. Prepare a fancy dinner with the best china and silverware. Have the kids dress up in their Sunday best and use the occasion to teach them proper etiquette.

6. Take your child through a mock interview for his or her first job.

7. Teach your children how to do their own laundry, iron their shirts or blouses, and keep their shoes shined.

8. Fathers, take your daughter through a fashion magazine and discuss modesty with her.

9. Have a mother/son date and a father/daughter date and use the occasion to coach appropriate actions and conversation. (This is good for preadolescents.)

10. Next time you see an umpire or official make a bad call, discuss with your children how the athletes either react or respond.

CHAPTER SEVEN

Discipline

The embossed seal of the United States Air Force gave the envelope a sense of importance. My misspelled name and address were scrawled on the front, while the return address yielded the name of a person I figured I'd never hear from again. Even though he was just starting his climb up the military ladder, the letters before and after his name gave his title a touch of prestige. Maybe miracles do happen.

There was no letter or card. Just a picture of a handsome and proud young man in his best Air Force blues. With the American flag for a backdrop and the ornaments of completed basic training on his chest and sleeve, I had to admit that he looked like a man with a future.

I turned the picture over and noticed a message. It simply said, "I told you!" It was not signed. It didn't need to be. The message was signature enough.

I'd only met him one time. That was enough for both of us. Actually, I'd spent the bulk of my time working with his parents by phone. We had met at a conference back East, and since I had spent some years working with teenagers, they thought I might have a few suggestions on how to deal with their son.

They treated me to lunch during a break in our schedules and it was then that I got my first look at their lives. Their car was the best. Their clothes were the best. Their address was the best. If I hadn't noticed, they would have told me. They told me everything.

They even told me how they came to be so "successful" (their word). They "lucked" into it. He was an eight-to-fiver, minding his own business and tinkering in his hobby shop in his free time. Then one of those ideas that makes everyone say, "Why didn't I think of that?" came along. He shared it with a franchiser and hasn't punched a clock since.

But the problem that brought us together was their boy. He was taking the joy out of their lives. He was flunking school, coming home drunk, sneaking out at night, and constantly getting into fights. They made more than their share of trips to the local precinct. They both admitted that they hated confrontation and that they gave in to him in order to avoid his rage. If he left, they'd be relieved, but they just couldn't kick him out. Besides, he was a minor and they could be held responsible for his mistakes.

In addition, they had their own set of problems. Their relationship had bumped over a lot of bad road since it started. They both fought battles with alcohol, weight, and the boundaries of morality. All their frustrations with the boy had accentuated their own damaged relationship. They had seriously considered splitting the wealth and the sheets down the middle and heading different directions.

It didn't take long to figure out that their lives lacked any discipline. And it was obvious they'd never worked up the sweat required to give any to their son. Without commitments to the pain of transparency, repentance, reconciliation, and accountability, there was little I could do. I was certain that the best they would offer was lip service to any plan suggested.

A couple of months later they called to say their son had been arrested. He had broken into a jewelry store and taken enough watches and brooches to put a smile on Liz Taylor. He hadn't made it two steps out the back door, however, before the police had nabbed him. Although he was a minor and this was his first major offense, the juvenile authorities informed his parents that they were going to delay his case until he was eighteen and then try him as an adult.

He was going to prison.

Such an awful thought moved his parents to belated action. They went to the jeweler and made a deal. They promised to return all the stolen items, repair the minor damage from the break-in, and make a mid-five-figure purchase—if the dealer would drop all charges. He agreed in a heartbeat and the boy was back on the street.

He was not going to prison.

"How could you do that?" I asked the parents. The mother started crying and told me it was the only way they could keep their boy from going to jail. She loved him, and couldn't bear the thought of him being locked up—not to mention all the horrible things that could happen to a young man in prison.

It was obvious by now they weren't calling for help. They wanted approval, and I couldn't give it to them. They were violating the laws of cause and effect, circumventing the consequences of actions, preempting the authority and discipline of the state. The big loser would be their son.

I agreed that it would be horrible for a kid to go to prison. If it were my son, I'd be devastated. But prisons are the logical destinations for those who choose illegal shortcuts. Jail is the University of Consequences for people who have been denied an education in discipline.

They thought I was harsh and uncaring and yelled at me loud enough to make me wonder if I *was* harsh and uncaring.

About six months later they called to say that their son was going to be flying through Phoenix. Would I be willing to talk with him? It turned out be the first and last time that I agreed to such a request.

I was surprised when I met him. He looked sharp, held his head high, was gracious and articulate. He sat down in my office and commented on its art and the pictures of my family on the wall. My first question concerned his relationship with his father.

"I love my dad. He's good to me. We don't always see eye-to-eye, but I think that has more to do with me growing up than anything else."

For ten minutes he spoke glowingly of his deep affection for his father. I tried the same question regarding his mother. Once again, I got broad, sweeping words of endearment. He sounded like a Mother's Day card, and for another ten minutes he told anecdotes and inside stories that emphasized his devotion to her.

My last question concerned his future: "What do you want to do?"

He came alive. Long before *Top Gun* he had wanted to be a fighter pilot, but since the release of the movie (which he had seen often enough to memorize), it was all that he thought about. As far as he was concerned, he wanted to spend the rest of his life "at Mach 2 with my hair on fire." He'd been to the recruiter. The paperwork was complete. He was going to ship out the day after graduation.

That was enough for me. I'm not the best at spotting a con job, but this one was too obvious. Once I started my little speech, I couldn't decide where to stop. I told him that he loathed his father, that he despised him for who he was and for what he had done to him. I told him that he didn't care much for his mother, either. She represented his inner struggle—she had been part of his problem—and his severe and exaggerated rebellion only demonstrated the deep-seated anger in his heart.

As I bit out my verdict, he sat up straighter, his jaw clenched tighter, and he leaned closer to the chair in which I sat.

I told him that fighter pilots don't flunk math and science. That the Air Force isn't going to put a twelve million dollar jet around a kid just because he thinks he's Tom Cruise.

In an instant he jumped to his feet with both fists clenched. My concern shifted from him to worrying about the shape and complexion of my face. It isn't Redford, but I didn't want this kid making any alterations. So I jumped to my feet.

I had anticipated his shove and braced for it. He didn't expect the return push and tripped over the coffee table that sits in front of the couch. He fell in a heap against the wall, and the force of his impact sent a picture crashing down first onto his shoulder, then his lap. It was a picture of Jesus holding a small child.

Neither one of us moved. We were both stunned. I sat on the edge of the table and looked at him until he broke the silence.

"My father never stood up to me like that."

"Well, you better get used to it," I said, not knowing what else to say, "you're going to get a lot more of it in the Air Force."

With that he got up, told me he was okay, said goodbye, and walked out. That was the last I heard of him or from him until I got his picture in the mail.

I told you so!

By the looks of the picture, he was right and I wasn't. Maybe he did have the stuff needed to make it in the Air Force. If so, I would be delighted to be proven wrong.

I've kept up with his life since I received his picture. And he is still in the armed services. However, you probably need to know that he's stationed . . .

. . . in Leavenworth Federal Penitentiary.

He's doing time for grand theft. His parents discovered that a military tribunal is not for sale.

No Shortcuts

It's hard to discuss discipline without getting negative. We can play mind games, believing that positive thinking will make life a cakewalk and assuming that a few kind words here and there will erase a painful or negligent past. But reality rejects that scenario.

There are no "happily-ever-after" guarantees. If we want the most out of life we must realize that there are no shortcuts around discipline. When it comes to passing on this gift to our children, our work seldom seems done.

Discipline helps children live up to their potential, their gifts, and their capabilities. It gives them a sense of confidence as they move into the future. Dreams more frequently come true for children who see that discipline consistently pays off.

The young man who walked into my office had all the raw potential, intelligence, and ability necessary to make it through life. Unfortunately, he hadn't submitted to the laws of discipline. He had never been forced to shape his potential in its crucible.

The legacy to our children will be tainted if we fail to put forth the effort necessary to develop habits of discipline. Now, I admit that of all of the aspects of a legacy of love, discipline causes me the greatest frustration. Its effects aren't immediately visible. My wife and I must continually remind our children, continually follow up on them, continually pray for them. Regardless of lessons taught, they never seem to see the value of daily habits.

That's why so many parents give up. Discipline is hard to quantify. It builds over a lifetime in small, hard-to-detect increments. We are so close to our children that we can't always see discipline developing.

My wife and I enjoy Western art. I realize that some people don't consider Western paintings "genuine art," but we do. Because we live in Scottsdale, Arizona, we are privileged to live near some of the finest Western art galleries in the world.

I don't think anyone hangs a better Western gallery than Troy Murray down on Main Street. He's a cowboy himself. He's *lived* those scenes. To hear him describe a picture makes you want to put on your chaps, don your Stetson and drive your station wagon off into the sunset. When he talks about a picture, you can taste the dust, smell the horses, and feel the heat.

It was at Troy's gallery that I got my first look at one of the masters of the old west. An original painting by Frederic Remington hung on the best wall in the place.

I like to study paintings up close. Seeing the brush strokes, the detail, the texture, makes me appreciate the work in a different way. It also makes me feel close to the artist. To think that *the* Frederic Remington touched this same canvas, mixed this exact shade of brown, used his palette knife on this cloud—you begin to feel very near to the man who once was.

But something else happens when you draw close. You see the touch-ups. The minute gaps between colors where the canvas shows through. The pencil marks where the artist sketched the picture. It's a completely different scene. When you're that close, looking with that much scrutiny, you see the flaws.

If you're not careful, you can lose confidence in the artist. You can imagine that he isn't as skilled as you once thought. If you aren't careful, you can lose confidence in art. You start to wonder if the Sistine chapel was paint-by-numbers or if Whistler's Mother was really his sister.

But when you step back far enough to take in the entire scene, the true beauty overwhelms you.

Transferring the skills of discipline to our children is something like that. It requires careful planning, a focus on the details, and keeping in mind the finished product. We can't let the mistakes of parents or children discourage us from making this skill into a permanent part of our children's makeup.

Unfortunately, our own battles with discipline sometimes discourage us from trying to build it into the lives of our sons and daughters. I have yet to meet parents who don't feel twinges of guilt as they look at their own lives. The mind, the mouth, the eyes, the waistline—they all give us plenty of reasons to doubt our qualifications for teaching our children about discipline.

We've got to keep in mind that building discipline, like building faith, integrity, or poise, is a *process*. It is the result of daily decisions and habits rehearsed over a lifetime. Each time we see discipline pay off we strengthen it as a character trait.

The Lifelong Benefit of Discipline

A seventy-year-old piano sits in our living room. I stripped and refinished the outside, and my friend Lonny (who's an expert on these things) tightened up everything on the inside. When it's dusted and polished it is an elegant addition to the decor.

But pianos were made to be played. They were uniquely designed to enrich the world with beautiful music. Several members of my family pride themselves on their ability at the ivories. I was a brass musician in high school and college and so never got a chance to study the piano. But I've memorized about six songs and my family has heard me play them several million times.

Karis is one who takes great pride in her skill at the piano. She's been taking lessons for two years and the family is starting to stick around when she practices. We even recognize most of the songs she plays.

Another family member also feels she has been graced with the heavenly gift of music. That's Shiloh, our two-year-old. She climbs up on the piano bench (whether you like it or not) and plays her infant concertos (whether you like it or not). I read somewhere that you shouldn't discourage this activity. I think it was written by some great pianist who never had any children.

Occasionally we're visited by folks who have spent decades perfecting their piano skills. They're at home with the keys, easily engaging our antique's seventy-year-old personality. When they play, the living room fills with the fruit of their years of discipline—beautiful, rich music.

What's the difference between my two-year-old and the friends with the honed skills?

Freedom.

That's the bottom line on discipline. In fact, it's the only way to win freedom. There is no freedom without discipline. You can't enjoy the benefits of freedom without paying a price. Arlington National Cemetery is proof of that.

Jesus said that truth will make us free. We embrace the truth by faith, demonstrate it through convictions, apply it with poise, and maintain it through discipline. When we are long gone and our children sit in the driver's seat of civilization, they will know that we loved them—*if* we pay the price today to give them the gift of discipline.

Lame Excuses—No Excuses

When you hear the swan songs of the defeated people around you, you quickly realize the critical place of discipline. Their solos begin as excuses and end up as indictments. Let me list a few of the standard lines of the defeated, undisciplined person:

. . . I didn't push my stool away from the bar.

. . . I put off doing my homework one too many times.

. . . I couldn't force myself to get out of bed in the morning.

. . . I couldn't get a grip on my anger.

. . . I neglected to follow up my prospects.

. . . I didn't spend enough time with my family because I couldn't walk away from work.

. . . I figured the problems would just solve themselves or go away.

. . . I just didn't take care of myself. I let myself go to seed.

. . . I acted on every urge I got.

. . . I couldn't keep my credit cards from controlling me.

Sound familiar? We've all heard such excuses, and we've spoken some of them. That's why we must refuse to back off from this responsibility to our children. I've seen the results of the downward slide enough to know that it's no way to run a life.

We don't want our children's marriages destroyed by ignorance of how to discipline their passions. Passions for money, passions for sex, passions for recognition, passions for control can finish off a family. A legacy of love demands that discipline be developed.

The Root of the Problem

Someone once defined discipline as "foregoing the immediate in order to guarantee the ultimate." It's saying no now in order to say yes later. When you run down the human checklist, there isn't a category that isn't radically benefited by discipline. Our bodies, our minds, our emotions, our spirits, our intellect, our relationships—regardless of the area, discipline allows us the freedom to maximize our capabilities.

But a nasty problem keeps us from developing disciplined lives. It's in all of us and doesn't need help to stay strong. It's naturally strong on its own.

It's laziness.

Take away its suffix and it's a four-letter word: L-A-Z-Y. It's as vile and profane a word as any in the gutter. Much of the human dilemma can be blamed on this simple, everyday word.

Laziness is sin, and those who fail to submit this vice to the redeeming work of Christ and the power of the Holy Spirit will find that it is indeed a vicious taskmaster.

If we want to move beyond a life of laziness and enjoy the freedom of discipline, we need to practice three principles simultaneously—the same three principles we must instill in our children if they are to enjoy discipline's life-long benefits.

Principle #1: Delayed gratification

"Delayed gratification is a process of scheduling the pain and pleasure of life in such a way as to enhance the pleasure by meeting and experiencing the pain first, and getting it over with. It is the only decent way to live."[7]

That's how Scott Peck put it in his fine book *The Road Less Traveled*. Peck says that laziness is behind every single case he's handled as a therapist.

Delayed gratification acknowledges that life has both pleasure and pain. You can't escape the pain, so why not schedule it?

The process of writing a book is a great lesson in delayed gratification. It's like writing a term paper every night for a year. Well, maybe not that bad. But there's some truth to the saying that writing a book "is like giving birth to barbed wire." It's a nasty grind. For me, however, it has been an excellent way to incorporate discipline into my life.

The better we parents get at scheduling our pain, the better equipped we are for teaching our children how to schedule theirs.

We are like coaches overseeing a group of athletes. Tom Landry, the former coach of the Dallas Cowboys, frequently sums up his job as a coach in an interesting way:

"I have a job to do that isn't that complicated, but it is often very difficult—to get a group of men to do what they don't want to do so that they can achieve what they've wanted all of their lives."

Our job as parents is to get our children to do what they don't want to do so that they can achieve what they've wanted all their lives—freedom, confidence, commitment, love.

Within the hearts of our children lie little kernels of discipline. They are dwarfed by the vines of laziness that are an innate part of human makeup. But if we fertilize those little kernels with the nutrients of delayed gratification, they will take root and sprout. In time they will grow with minimal maintenance.

A commitment to delayed gratification, instilled in the early years, can keep our kids from succumbing to illicit sex and will reward them with a wonderful, pure, lifelong sexual relationship with a marriage partner.

Delayed gratification will prepare our kids for the dog days of college and graduate school when they have to forego sleep and money in order to get the credentials they need to compete. It will help them accept the entry-level job in order to earn their way to their potential.

Delayed gratification will keep them from becoming enslaved to deceptive cards of plastic resting in their wallets.

But if delayed gratification is to help construct a disciplined life, it needs an ally.

Principle #2: Advanced decision-making

Many battles in life are won or lost before we ever enter the battlefield.

A teenaged girl won't win her battle with passion after she's already climbed into the backseat. A teenaged boy won't win his battle with lust after he's bought the dirty magazine. We won't maintain conditioned, healthy bodies if we don't make some decisions in advance. We have to understand exactly what we want in order to organize our options.

Such planning doesn't ruin spontaneity, it accentuates it. It sets us free to do the things we otherwise wouldn't.

Advanced decision-making appears on our calendars when we mark out dates for spouse and children in order to prevent the attractive demands of our cluttered culture from getting in the way.

But even this is not enough. One final element is vital to the disciplined life. We need:

Principle #3: A focused goal

A focused goal answers the question, "Why?" Children

want to know *why* discipline is necessary—what's in it for them? The reasons we give them must be big enough.

One of these big reasons is to avoid the *other* kind of discipline. Good parents know how to administer appropriate doses of discomfort to appropriate parts of the anatomy. But negative reinforcement only goes so far. The practiced life of discipline must come from motivations rooted deep in the soul.

Every four years people across the world huddle around their TV sets to watch the greatest athletes in the world compete in the Olympic Games. We see the risks, the sweat, and the sacrifices culminate in photo finishes. Winners get their moment of glory on the victor's stand and a gold medal to store in their safety deposit box.

There's a good chance that the apostle Paul saw something like the Olympic Games. When he speaks about discipline he uses the races as a metaphor. I like to imagine the crowd screaming in the background as I read his words in 1 Corinthians. Listen to this godly man's advice:

> Do you not know that in a race all the runners run, but only one gets the prize? Run in such a way as to get the prize. Everyone who competes in the games goes into strict training. They do it to get a crown that will not last; but we do it to get a crown that will last forever [A Focused Goal]. Therefore I do not run like a man running aimlessly [Advanced Decision Making]; I do not fight like a man beating the air. No, I beat my body and make it my slave [Delayed Gratification] so that after I have preached to others, I myself will not be disqualified for the prize (9:24-27, NIV).

Our children are a "big enough why" for us. They are worth the exasperation, the repeated requests, the consistent mistakes, the anger, the tears, the sweat, the worry, the heartache, and the embarrassment. Add up all the liabilities that go with developing discipline in their lives, and they are still worth it.

They are worth it to us because we were worth it to God. He had a price to pay, too. He could have listed legitimate excuses why He shouldn't bother making the sacrifice. But He did make it. Some of the sweetest words in the Bible are found near the end of the book of Hebrews. Its twelfth chapter describes the beauty of discipline and encourages us to hand this legacy to our children:

> Therefore, since we have so great a cloud of witnesses surrounding us [our children], let us also lay aside every encumbrance, and the sin which so easily entangles us, and let us run with endurance the race that is set before us, fixing our eyes on Jesus, the author and perfecter of faith, who for the joy set before Him endured the cross, despising the shame, and has sat down at the right hand of the throne of God (vv. 1-2).

We were the joy set before Him. *We* were His "big enough why." We are the recipients of His legacy of love . . . and He calls us to pass it on.

As you read these words there's a young, undisciplined man holed up in the corner of a smothering Leavenworth cell. He's there because his parents sent him into adulthood unequipped for the pressures of life—pressures that can only be defeated with discipline.

It didn't have to be.

You and I are the best insurance policies our children have against such a plight. When we weave into the legacy of their lives a commitment to discipline, we will truly set their spirits free.

And Leavenworth will be a million miles away.

TEN WAYS TO TEACH YOUR CHILD DISCIPLINE

1. Take your children to juvenile court to listen to some cases. Afterward take them out for a soda and discuss the subject of "consequences."

2. Have them study a musical instrument (regardless of whether they have any musical aptitude) long enough to learn about the discipline of practice.

3. Enroll them in a team sport where their faithful attendance and participation is required.

4. Assign daily chores and hold them responsible to perform them (make their bed, pick up their clothes, set the table, etc.).

5. Have them tithe every Sunday from their allowance.

6. Make sure that they complete homework.

7. Have them write to a missionary once a month.

8. Give them an alarm clock, show them how to use it, and have them assume the responsibility of getting up on time for school *for a whole year!* If they are late because they failed to get up, don't write them an excuse (that circumvents consequences). Let the school principal give them some good reasons why they ought to get to school on time.

9. Help them memorize an elaborate poem.

10. Take them to a junkyard and show them the wreckage of cars involved in alcohol-related accidents.

CHAPTER EIGHT

Endurance

The world is filled with wide-eyed, idealistic starters, but painfully lacking in determined finishers.

That's the difference between discipline and endurance. Discipline gets people going. Endurance enables them to go the distance.

On the first Sunday in November, America gets a chance to tune in to one of the greatest illustrations of life the sporting world has ever devised. That's when nineteen thousand men and women gather on Staten Island to run the New York City Marathon.

I'm awed by this spectacle for two reasons. First, it marks the culmination of months of training and sacrifice. That is admirable. Second, these nineteen thousand people huddled at the starting line are going to run twenty-six miles, three hundred eighty-five yards through *New York City*. Anyone who thinks there is safety in numbers hasn't been to the Bronx lately. The *cab ride* from Staten Island to Central Park is dangerous enough. These brave souls are taking on the five boroughs of New York *on foot*.

The Big Apple marathon is more than just a test of conditioning; it's a lesson in survival. Only the resolute will make it to the end.

I'm a vicarious marathoner. That means I have absolutely no intention of ever running one. But I take great delight in watching other people push their bodies to the limit.

My friend Mark Holmlund actually did it. Don't bother getting out your marathoner's almanac. He's not listed among the select few who dominate the upper echelons of this sport. He's one of those "also rans" whose record of their participation is extremely personal. It was recorded in his mind, his feet, his back, his stomach, his calves, his arms, and his thighs. Before it was over, every cell in his body knew that he had run the New York City Marathon.

Mark was twenty-four, fresh out of graduate school, and one of the newest members of the Merrill Lynch team. He was in New York completing his in-house training before he would take his assignment on the West Coast. Maybe it was the fact that he was young, maybe it was the fact that he was single, or maybe it was just some deep-seated death wish that motivated him to sign up. Regardless, at 5:30 A.M. on the morning of the race he left the safety of his apartment and walked through the cool darkness of a New York City morning to board a bus at the library on 42nd Street.

That's when Mark got his first hint of the magnitude of this event. Dozens of buses groaned by the curbs as thousands of athletes boarded them for their shuttle ride to Staten Island.

He arrived at the starting line by 6:30. That left him three-and-a-half hours to stand around wondering what cerebral short-circuit had provoked him to attempt a stunt like this. All the distractions, however, didn't allow much time to reconsider. Aerobics instructors on elevated stands led stretching exercises. Harried assistants poured gallons of green Gatorade. Banners flew, bands played, concessionaires barked their wares, and Mayor Ed Koch gave a speech. It was a happening, and it was all New York.

As the runners lined up, Mark had a choice. He could take rank in the fast men's line. Those are the ones who will finish in less than two hours and forty minutes. Then there is the fast women's line. They also set a blurring pace. First-time participants are supposed to line up behind the women. But Mark wasn't behaving normally in the first place. He'd signed up for this crazy race, so why not do something equally insane and take his stand among the fleetest of the fleet?

He did. The gun sounded.

In about two seconds Mark realized he was in the wrong group. He was a couple hundred bodies deep in a stampede of running shoes and pointed elbows. If he fell, he'd be lucky if they found him tomorrow. Before he crossed the Verrazano Narrows Bridge, barely a mile into the race, he had already used up five miles' worth of energy. The slight incline of the bridge seemed like a mountain. But it was either run or die.

In Brooklyn, the pack spread out. In Queens, children handed him fruit and juice. Old ladies hung out apartment windows cheering him on. Bearded, black-clothed Hasidic Jews debated eternal issues as he ran down their streets.

Suddenly, things were looking up. This is what he had signed up for. This was running and New York at its finest. He was exhilarated. He was on top of his race, on top of his world.

On the Queensboro Bridge into Manhattan, he ran into a stiff wind. He locked his chin down and leaned into the pressure.

It was just over the bridge, just past mile eighteen, just as he started to head up 1st Avenue, just as he got into the middle of a thoroughfare lined with a million people, that an invisible enemy stepped out in front of him.

An abrupt feeling of cold shock surrounded him. A screaming voice inside him shouted, "You're done!"

Runners call it "the Wall." And Mark hit it in full stride right in front of all those people.

This is where endurance separates the starters from the finishers. This is where the inner man discusses with the outer man what's going to happen to the ultimate man. Mark still had eight miles to go—most of them through Harlem and the Bronx.

He managed to keep leaning forward for the next eight miles. He didn't realize that the wall he slapped up against was actually his body shifting into a hypoglycemic state. He gorged himself with bananas while craving chocolate ice cream.

He went through Harlem, made a token appearance in the Bronx, came back into Harlem and finally slipped into Central Park running parallel with 5th Avenue. Tourists pay top dollar to come to this exact spot—to walk down the avenue of the most famous hotels in the world. But Mark didn't notice the Plaza, the Sherry Netherland, or the Pierre. He didn't take in the haunting beauty of Central Park set against the stark magnitude of Manhattan. All he wanted to see was the banner that said "Finish Line" in front of Tavern on the Green.

A right off of 5th and onto 59th marked the beginning of the end. When he took that right turn and headed north for the last three hundred yards of the New York City Marathon, one singular thought burned a hole in the deepest recesses of his brain . . .

. . . *Golf.*

I'm going to take up golf.

I will never again allow my ego to talk me into doing anything like this. Ever.

Hitting the Wall

Rearing a family is a marathon. And managing to leave a legacy of love is a marathon within a marathon. We hit enough walls just trying to get our children from the delivery room to college. But if we want to pass on eternal character traits along the way, we're going to hit walls every day.

That's why endurance must be a part of our personal makeup as well as one of the character traits we want to hand off to our children. It's that step beyond discipline that keeps us going when we'd rather just quit.

Communities throughout our country are filled with sad and empty parents who decided that the finish line was too far away and that the race wasn't worth it. They pulled out of the pack, slipped down a side street, and lost themselves in the back alleys of their careers, hobbies, and causes. When they saw how far they had to go and how painfully difficult it was going to be to make it to the home stretch, they calculated their options and gave up.

I've been in many of these homes. I've listened to the parents as they salve their wounded spirits with rationalizations. And looking at the obstacles they were dealing with, I've been forced to admit that I could be as inclined to give up as they were.

Some people hit the wall called "Money." They simply can't get the right kind of work needed to supply the minimal needs of their family. With both Dad and Mom working extended hours, there's still not enough to go around.

Some people hit the wall called "In-laws." No matter how hard they try, these couples can't seem to please their parents. The bride and bridegroom were more than willing to sever the umbilical cord of dependence on their parents, more than ready to "leave and cleave." All they wanted from Mom and Dad was a blessing. Instead they got relentless manipulations and power plays.

Some people smack into a wall called "The Boss." It's that subtle but certain way he waves a paycheck under their nose. It's that convicting "be-a-team-player" speech that convinces them the family must yield the right-of-way.

Some people run into the wall called "Comparison." They can't escape the pace and style of their peers, and the more they size themselves up against the competition, the more they realize how far behind they are.

Tim and Darcy Kimmel have hit some walls. The marathon of parenting can get to any of us. Our intentions are noble, our checklists thorough, and our actions sincere, but right in the middle of a great pace—we hit it. Maybe it's a manipulative friend, an unforeseen expense, a physical setback, or just the grinding, run-of-the-mill frustrations that occur when two selfish adults are trying to raise three selfish children.

Sometimes we just want to give up. The voice screaming inside of us makes a lot of convincing arguments:

"If that kid doesn't want to learn character, that's his problem."

"It doesn't matter, they'll never change."

"These little bandits couldn't care less that I worked my can off all day just so they could have three squares and a bed."

"You can talk, you can plead, and you can beg, but they're not going to listen."

"What's the use in trying to instill this elaborate moral code in them? Some pimply-faced jerk is going to come along and sweet-talk them out of it anyway."

Our walls may not be anything like your walls. It doesn't really matter. Once you've run full tilt into unyielding mortar and stone, you're not really concerned with particulars. Whenever we find ourselves making excuses for giving up, we need to muster the endurance to keep with it.

Fortunately, God gives us regular opportunities to regroup. For Darcy and me, our main opportunity for relief comes about 9:00 at night, a half-hour after our children have gone to bed. By that time they've dropped into that deep, sweet, coma-like sleep that young children get to enjoy. And as you stand there at the foot of their beds, you see the reasons why you can't give up. You see how fragile, how defenseless, how dependent they are. You remember that they're just children. We can't expect them to be mature. They don't have an adult emotional system. They're *children*—potential leaders or followers in little bodies.

God throws breathers into our day. Just when we figured our child has no capacity for manners, he says "please" and "thank you" to his *sister*. About the time we conclude our child has no bent toward spiritual things, we see her bow her head and thank God out loud for creating butterflies. Those little holes in the wall give us hope. We get a little more confidence in our pace and a little more energy in our step.

Don't Try to Set Any Records

We'd all be a lot better off if we'd stop trying to set records as parents and simply concentrate our efforts on *finishing.* That's the biggest challenge of a marathon. That's why we're impressed when a person crosses the finish line.

Character is hard to measure. So is maturity. For one thing, they escape easy definitions. They don't submit to syllogistic arguments that say if you do A and then add B, you'll get C every time. That's why endurance has to be a daily part of our strategy for parenting.

Faith is a lifelong journey. Integrity must be sustained to the grave. Poise is a series of daily choices. Discipline is the accumulation and maintenance of healthy habits.

These traits don't come cheaply. They are forged in the heat of stress and the pressure of loneliness. When Mark Holmlund ran the New York City Marathon, he felt utterly alone. Even though he was surrounded by thousands of other runners, he knew that none of them was going to be able to cross the finish line on his behalf. If he was going to officially make it to the Tavern on the Green, he was going to have to run twenty-six miles, three hundred eighty-five yards.

Enduring to the End

If we got out our Greek lexicons and chased down the essence of the word "endurance," we'd find that it's actually a compound word meaning *under life.* It doesn't take a scholar to figure out what that means. Endurance is the ability to hold up under the weight of daily living. To hang in rather than merely hang on.

There are five steps that can help us maintain a life pattern of endurance. But if we want to leave a legacy of love we have to do more than simply appropriate these into our lives—we must transfer them into our children.

1. Set goals

Daily life is far more tolerable when we consistently compare it to the "Big Picture." Endurance has to have a goal. If we believe that what we are doing is futile, we are more inclined to quit.

Some parents set up their children to be quitters by establishing arbitrary goals that have no ultimate meaning. Let me give you an example.

Grades on a report card are important. In some ways they are a measurement of progress, an indicator of where a student needs to improve. However, they can just as easily be an extension of the parents' ego. Parents can try to use their children's grades as a measurement of *themselves*. They figure, "If my kid is making great grades, I must be doing a good job." Straight A's make great copy on the Christmas newsletter and look good in the family album.

Motivating children to go after the grades rather than the knowledge and skills those grades measure is a shaky goal at best. Such an incentive isn't attractive enough to keep tired legs churning once little bodies hit the wall. The motivation of "grades for grades' sake" will stop kids cold when the only way to prepare for a test is to stay up half of the night. Why bother? What difference does it make? Unless our children see a big "Why" for losing sleep to prepare for an exam, it will be too easy to shut out the light. Grades for grades' sake also make cheating an attractive option. If it's not the content, but the letter on the card that really counts, why not utilize the easiest method?

We need to maintain goals that make sense—goals that enable us to relate our present activity to ultimate and worthy ends. Changing diapers, washing clothes, keeping the car repaired, and all the other mundane parts of daily life could seem meaningless if we aren't careful. But when we see them as service to eternal, dearly loved people, the tasks seem a lot more tolerable.

The world scoffs at a mother because she serves the domestic needs of her family rather than pursuing the glamour and glitz of a female exec. It's all a question of ultimate goals. That mom can't take a gold watch or stock certificate with her to heaven. But she can take her children.

The goal of leaving a legacy of love lies in the distance. It's a wonderful finish line. But because it's out there so far and there are so many excuses that could keep us from getting there, we need to employ a second step to help us endure.

2. Break goals into manageable moments

Mark Holmlund ran his course a borough at a time, a bridge at a time, and a block at a time. Hills needed one pace, flat stretches another.

We need to build our children's sense of faith. They don't have to memorize the entire New Testament before they're ten. When they have a problem, we don't need to recite volumes of systematic theology. We need to break their spiritual development into manageable moments—realizing all along that we are not the Holy Spirit. He'll manage much better if we don't choke our children with the truth.

Every area of their lives can be broken into manageable moments. One problem a lot of dads have when working with their children in sports is to miscalculate things like strength, size, and stamina. They demand adult performance from little bodies. That's not unfortunate—that's sin. It happens when we focus on performance (a terminal goal), rather than on the character and skill that can ultimately benefit a child later in life (a relational goal). Building character and strong bonds between parent and child is far more important than home runs or touchdowns.

Don't misunderstand. I'm not saying that children never need to be pushed in a certain direction. Their instinctive bent toward laziness demands that we sometimes set higher goals and standards for them than they might choose to pursue. We simply need to make sure that those goals are reasonable and safe.

Manageable moments are good for our marriage, our relationship with God, and our relationship with friends. Endurance is far more achievable when we run our race through life at a tolerable pace.

3. Make trials your friend

I've met people who actually assume they can live out their lives in a hassle-free environment—some kind of hermetically sealed bubble. They don't assume the occasional headaches or make allowances for the inevitable setbacks. As a result, obstacles wipe them out instead of just tripping them up. They hit a wall and shatter in a thousand pieces.

I get a kick out of watching new parents. Especially those who married later in life or were married for several years before they had children (Darcy and I had to wait eight years before we conceived our first). Their lives are suddenly and permanently turned inside out. They were used to sleeping in when they needed rest or getting to bed early when their bodies cried out for sleep. Surprise! Bring home your first kid and you don't feel adequately rested for the next twenty years. That's kids! That's life! And that's not so bad.

Once we wake up to the reality that . . .

LIFE IS DIFFICULT

. . . then we can go about the business of getting important things done. Many families have been destroyed because a dad or mom couldn't accept the fact that having children requires trade-offs.

For eight years I had the discretionary time and extra money to be able to play golf every week. Then we brought Karis home from the hospital. In a matter of weeks she was cognizant of my presence and my absence. Even before we had Cody I realized that with the limited free time I had, and the brief number of years the kids came under our influence, it was going to be difficult to carve out five hours each Saturday to putter around a golf course. Life is difficult. Priorities require trade-offs. Saturday golf had to go.

I'm working on a legacy of love instead of my handicap. Lord willing, I'll have plenty of time after the kids have grown to take a few strokes off of my game.

It's easier to make those kinds of decisions when you realize . . .

THE DIFFICULTIES IN LIFE ARE PUT THERE TO MAKE US STRONG.

James put it like this:

Consider it all joy, my brethren, when you encounter various trials, knowing that the testing of your faith produces endurance. And let endurance have its perfect result, that you may be perfect and complete, lacking in nothing (James 1:2-4).

The easy life doesn't require faith, integrity, strength, or sacrifice. But a life worth living does. A life worth living produces a legacy worth leaving, and our sweat is a symbol to our kids that love takes hard work.

We can be better equipped to gain strength from our trials if we . . .

BELIEVE THAT THE DIFFICULTIES WE ENCOUNTER COME FROM A HEAVENLY FATHER WHO LOVES US.

Again, James suggests what to do when the pressures of life take their toll.

But if any of you lacks wisdom, let him ask of God, who gives to all men generously and without reproach, and it will be given to him (James 1:5).

When those infants keep waking up in the middle of the night . . . ask God for help.

When those toddlers keep wetting their training pants . . . ask God for help.

When those elementary school children keep fighting over the Nintendo game—take it away from them . . . and ask God for help.

When those junior highers won't get off the phone . . . ask God for help.

When those high schoolers won't come in on time . . . ask God for help.

When those college students don't call . . . ask God for help.

When those newlyweds finally drive off from the reception . . . thank God for the help!

Realize that nothing is going to touch your life that doesn't first pass through the filter of God's love. Darcy and I are friends with three different couples who at this writing each have daughters who are battling leukemia. None of these friends takes a pill called "God" that makes the pain go away. They know full well the agony of waiting . . . the frustration of helplessness. But they all testify to the soothing sense of God's presence as they face the same dark, unyielding wall.

They know that endurance is a process. It's a muscle that must stay flexed for long periods of time. And when there's nothing left in them, that's when they feel the presence of God the most . . . holding them up, carrying them along.

4. Crash through the quitting points

We all face times when a million excuses crowd our minds. At such moments, we wonder if we can complete this marathon called parenting. It's at these critical junctures—when we hit that emotional, intellectual, physical, or spiritual wall—that we need to consciously weigh our options. Our brains need to review the facts:

. . . I have a goal

. . . it's broken into manageable moments

. . . I'm not afraid of trials

. . . they're my friends

. . . they're part of life

. . . they make me strong

. . . my loving Heavenly Father wouldn't allow them if He didn't think I could handle them

. . . I can't stop now, my children are too important

. . . crash through!

I'm not playing positive mind games here. I'm not pretending all the pain and hurt and frustration will go away. I am simply acknowledging that endurance requires us to face our obstacles honestly, acknowledge them for what they are, and in God's strength, crash through them. Quitting points must be aggressively attacked, fought, and defeated. That's endurance.

Our spouse can help at these crucial points. Leaving a legacy of love sometimes requires us to hand the baton off to our mate. When fatigue, discouragement, fear, or anger start to get the best of us, we need to reach out for help to make it through the wall.

That brings up a final step we need to take in order to maintain endurance.

5. Surround yourself with conquerors rather than quitters

Endurance is a lot easier when it is the standard operating procedure of the people with whom you spend most of your time. You and I believe our kids will make better decisions if they spend their childhood watching us make good decisions. We believe their behavior is affected by the company they keep. The same principles apply to Moms and Dads! If bad company isn't a good idea for them, it isn't for us either.

We need to make sure that the "significant others" in our lives are the kind of people who model endurance. They need to be people with a good track record.

When I play tennis, I always want to play someone who has superior skills. I don't improve when I can easily beat my opponent (in fact, I regress). I want to play someone who makes me work hard, concentrate, maximize strategy. I want him to do his best. Then, when I've reached a little deeper inside of me, made greater demands on my body, run the limits of my court strategy and *beat* him (or at least take a game), I can enjoy the thrill of knowing that walls are not impenetrable.

Whether it's the game of tennis or the struggle of parenting, we all do better when we have a circle of friends who make a habit of enduring.

Some of you reading this book are raising your children solo. Death or the divorce judge has left you on your own. For you, this point is non-negotiable. Without strong, encouraging friends, you're going to have a difficult time penetrating the walls.

Don't forget that you always have the Lord. Spending time with Him the first thing each morning is a lifesaving habit for you and a priceless example to your family. By making Him the first focus of your day, you are more likely to turn to Him when you hit your quitting points.

Our partners can play a key role in our quest for endurance. We can build the character trait of endurance into our children by first building it into our marriage. Sometimes, however, we may have to be on the teaching end of the learning curve. It may not be pretty, but it's worth it.

I remember one particular afternoon a number of years ago when I dragged myself home from the office. I'd been out of town, had stopped by the office to pick up the mail, then came home.

Because it was a few hours before dinner, Darcy suggested that we take Karis (who was only one at the time) out for a treat. I wasn't excited about the idea, but when Darcy loaded the baby in the car and handed me the keys, I got the feeling that my opinion wasn't part of the equation.

We ended up taking her to a Dairy Queen crowded with screaming school children. I'd just come from a three-day conference where I had spoken to a crowd of screaming school children. I didn't feel well. My head hurt. My eyes hurt. My hair hurt. But there we were, and there we sat.

They served our ice cream quickly enough, and I figured that the sooner we finished it off, the sooner we'd be out of the joint. But one-year-old kids have no concept of time. And it didn't take long for me to realize that they don't have any concept of ice cream, either. It's supposed to go *in* their face, not *on* it.

Karis was a mess. What's worse, she seemed to be enjoying it. She smeared it in her hair, up her arms, under her arms, and all over the front of her outfit.

Another thing that ticked me off was that Darcy didn't seem to think anything unusual was going on. The way she kept talking and laughing at Karis, I could have sworn she was *encouraging* the behavior.

I finished my ice cream and waited. Kids kept screaming and running all over the place, my wife kept giggling and jabbering at the baby, and Karis kept layering herself with goo. Then came the last straw. Somehow, Karis managed to flip a blob of ice cream halfway across the table from her plastic spoon to my sleeve.

That was it. Time's up. Show's over.

I jumped up, started wiping my sleeve with a napkin, and snarled at my wife. "Get her cleaned up, Darcy, we're leaving. I'm not having any fun!"

She continued playing with Karis, looked up at me with one of those looks and said . . .

"We're not here for *you,* we're here for *her.*"

I looked down at my daughter. She was smiling up at me through her ice cream—unaware that I wasn't having any fun. God melted my heart as thoroughly as time melted the ice cream on her face. He used Karis's look and my godly wife's words to convict my selfish heart. Darcy reached over, touched my hand, and put an it's-okay-to-be-wrong-occasionally-just-don't-stay-that-way expression in place of that *other* one and smiled.

Somehow, Darcy had managed to look past the inconvenience, the noise, and the mess. She saw something bigger and finer in that moment—something I had missed in my impatience. It wouldn't always be "just the three of us" eating ice cream together on a summer afternoon. We wouldn't always have a one-year-old girl with chocolate syrup in her hair. She also knew that if I just tried, I could muster the strength I needed to maximize the moment.

Gently but firmly, she boosted me over my wall.

TEN WAYS TO TEACH YOUR CHILDREN ENDURANCE

1. Discuss one of their unfinished personal projects, and then help them set a goal to finish.

2. Take a twenty-mile bicycle trip in one day.

3. Purchase a complicated model and set a time limit to have it done.

4. Have them read a classic in a reasonable time limit. Establish a reward for them when they are done.

5. Take them on a nature hike and discuss the plants that endure through cold winters and hot summers.

6. Read them the book *The Miracle Worker.*

7. Take them on a hike over rugged but safe terrain.

8. Have an accomplished musician or athlete talk with them about endurance.

9. Visit a physical therapy ward where people are having to learn to walk over again.

10. Open a savings account. Have them save a certain sum of money that you agree to match once they meet their goal.

CHAPTER NINE

Courage

Plastered over one special wall in our house is a montage of snapshots and formal portraits. On that wall you'll find pictures of people still here and people who have gone ahead, pictures of me in my thinner years and pictures of Darcy in her . . . younger years. Pictures of the kids. Pictures of the relatives. Pictures of friends of the family.

Through the years this gallery has grown to include scores of moments and memories. Somewhere along the way it picked up the nickname "The Wall of Fame." But you don't have to do anything more famous than catch a fish, pose with Mickey Mouse, or get a new set of roller skates to gain a prominent spot.

I suppose visitors consider it an eyesore and wonder how we keep it dusted (we don't). But it's not there for decoration. Its lack of esthetic appeal is of no concern to

Darcy and me. We just love the people in the pictures and want to be reminded of them every day.

Three Portraits

Let me dust off three frames for you. They've hung there for quite some time. They're part of the "permanent collection." The people looking out of these three frames have taught me a lot.

The first picture needs some explanation. It's not your typical photograph. It's a picture of a dear friend, but he didn't give it to me. I found it one afternoon when I was rooting around in an antique store. Some old *Life* magazines were laying in a cardboard box, and as I leafed through the pile his picture stared out at me from one of the front covers. Before I mention his name, I need to tell you how we met.

After I graduated from seminary, Darcy and I came to Scottsdale to serve a church. This man and his wonderful wife always sat up front. He wore a constant smile, had a contagious personality, and talked in anecdotes. I usually had something to do during the Sunday morning services so I normally sat up front. That's how we got to know each other. Since then, our relationship with Joe and Didi has been cemented through several hunting and fishing trips and a decade of holiday dinners.

I mentioned his name, Joe. More specifically, Joe Foss. The date on the *Life* magazine is June 7, 1943. That's the White House behind him. That's a Marine aviator's uniform he's wearing. And that's the Congressional Medal of Honor hung around his neck. When the picture was taken, he had just walked out of the Oval Office where President Roosevelt had read a citation from Congress and then strung the medal around his collar.

If you looked up courage in the dictionary, it wouldn't be surprising to find a picture of Joe next to the definition.

He was one of the greatest heroes of World War II. That's why he got the Congressional Medal of Honor. It's not some merit badge. The Congressional Medal of Honor is the highest tribute that our country can bestow upon a member of the military. Most of those who earned it had it presented posthumously.

I'm thankful Joe was able to receive his in person.

He earned it flying combat missions in the vicinity of Guadalcanal. As squadron leader, he daily led his men into battle. They attacked Japanese convoys and provided air support for American troops fighting to regain the islands of the South Pacific.

But their greatest challenge was securing hostile skies dotted with one of the deadliest weapons Japan ever created—the famous "Zero" fighters. Few were the days Joe didn't engage one of Japan's best. Twice they shot him down. Once he landed with a Zero's cannons tearing into his plane.

Still, Joe sent far more of them flaming out of the sky than vice versa. He wasn't trying to set a record, but he did. By the time all the smoke had cleared over Guadalcanal, Joe had shot down twenty-six Japanese planes—a feat unsurpassed by any American before or since.

There's another picture hanging on our "Wall of Fame." The man in this photo also wears a uniform. His picture, however, isn't from the pages of *Life* magazine. It's from the pages of my life.

He's my father.

No medals hang around his neck. His uniform is standard Government Issue. And the patch on his sleeve wouldn't prompt a salute from anybody. But he was, nonetheless, a man of courage.

Dad was a member of the 10th Armored Division assigned to the Third Army, General George S. Patton, commander. By the time Dad joined the division in Europe, this elite group had won back most of France. Hitler and the Germans were on the run.

In late September 1944, Dad stepped from a ship's gangplank and into Cherbourg, France. After several weeks of restless preparation, his division was finally on wheels and mobilized. On All Saints' Day they met up with the Made-In-The-U.S.A. Army that was giving the Nazis so many migraines. They arrived in time to assist in the capture of Metz.

Before the war, my father was an apprentice machinist and a topflight mechanic. It was these skills which got him assigned to the mobile armored division. His job was to keep everything that had wheels, moving. It would have been a relatively safe job if not for the Germans' last desperate offensive.

History remembers it as the "Battle of the Bulge," and because of it, Dad found himself within spitting distance of the enemy more often than he would have preferred.

He celebrated Christmas that year hip-deep in snow just outside of Bastogne. He ate a full course turkey dinner while firing a 105 mm. howitzer against enemy positions in and around the town (Merry Christmas, Adolf!).

The weary and depleted German army couldn't take the ferocious pounding served up by the Allies. By mid-January they were in retreat, and by the middle of spring it was over. On May 8, 1945, General Eisenhower's assistant accepted the treaty of unconditional surrender from the German leadership. The next day Dad and his outfit celebrated in Garmisch-Partenkirchen. That date was important to Dad. It not only meant he could go home, but it was the birthday of his main reason for wanting a ticket on the first ship home.

That's her in the third frame. The picture was taken shortly after she and Dad were married. Mom had grown up in a little bend in the road just outside of New Castle,

Pennsylvania. She and Dad met on the playground as kids, fell in love as teenagers, and married as young adults. About a year after she posed for the photo, Dad shipped out. And while he and his division were making their way to Metz, she gave birth to their first child.

Like everybody else during the war, Mom did her part. She rebuilt generators and starters for military equipment. In addition she nurtured my oldest brother through his first year. When I think of her life, I realize that she, too, was a woman of great courage.

When Dad was discharged from the Army at Indiantown Gap, Pennsylvania, Mom was there to meet him—two among the millions throughout the country who were being reunited after the long and bitter years of war.

The courage they demonstrated during the war would represent but a small fraction of what they'd need throughout their married years. Why? Because they ultimately ended up the parents of six children.

In the decades that followed they would have to make heavy withdrawals at the bank of courage in order to stare down and vanquish the enemies that would try to steal away the future of six impressionable kids. Defeat would be waiting at every slip. It was sheer resolve that kept them from buckling under the pressure. They would need courage. . .

   . . . to look at six kids and then look into an empty refrigerator

   . . . to stay awake long after their energy had played out in order to apply a fresh mustard plaster to a sleepless, coughing child

   . . . to watch doctor after doctor sew up cut after cut

   . . . to be toyed with by fickle economies and yet consistently succeed by expending more sweat

. . . to listen to neighbors complain about their noisy, frustrating kids, and know that their neighbors were right

. . . to watch their children struggle to win and not intervene to assure their victory

. . . to see to it that six kids were fed, bathed, dressed, and in the third pew on the left each Sunday by the time the first hymn was sung

. . . to stop by a bedroom and kiss a sleeping child's forehead despite day-long disobedience

. . . to maintain a workable relationship of mutual trust with their children despite not always believing every word they said

. . . to watch them leave one by one, wondering if the idealism that each carried would stand up to the relentless challenges of reality.

My parents didn't get any special citations from FDR. The only household where they enjoyed name recognition was their own. And yet their actions in the trenches of the home earned them medals of honor. Six, to be exact. And they wore them and continue to wear them with quiet pride.

The courage that hurled Joe Foss into the flaming guns of a Japanese fighter pilot . . . that Howard Kimmel drew upon to steady himself for his work while enemy bombs fell around him . . . that Winifred Kimmel revealed as she rocked her son through the cold, lonely Pennsylvania winter of 1944, is the same courage that we need in order to face today and tomorrow.

These people were courageous not because they had some uncommon gift, but because they tapped the resources of courage within them. We decorate men like Joe Foss because he willingly climbed into the cockpit of his airplane despite the good chance he wouldn't come back. We welcome back men like my father because he dedicated himself to unapplauded services needed to keep heroes doing what heroes do. We admire people like my mother because she didn't begrudge life for being unfair, unpredictable, and normal.

The Missing Link

As I observe the eroding foundations of the American family, I am convinced that most of the devastation can be traced to a fundamental shortage of parental courage. The cracks in the walls of a typical family might appear to stem from a spiritual, moral, intellectual, emotional, or physical problem, but the majority might have been prevented if parents had been willing to exercise courage.

That makes courage a vital component of the formula for a legacy of love.

We have to have faith, but I know people whose faith has failed because they refused to muster enough courage to make it work.

We have to have integrity, but the world is filled with people of the highest convictions who have fallen in the face of temptation because they didn't have courage to turn away.

We have to maintain a poised and balanced life-style, but for lack of courage good people have become notorious examples of the inappropriate.

We have to have discipline, yet we all know folks who have walked away from the starting blocks because starting assumed finishing, and that demanded more courage than they were willing to exercise.

We have to have endurance, but we've all seen people who gave up when the pressures of those final laps around their God-given responsibilities became too great.

I don't have to look very far for examples of these kinds of people. Usually a mirror is all that I need. I'm just like the next guy; I'm only a moment away from my next challenge. Because life is lived by the second, we can move from winners to losers in a heartbeat.

Joe Foss will tell you. It took courage for him to lay his life on the line enough times to shoot down twenty-six enemy planes. It also took courage for him to humbly receive the Congressional Medal of Honor from the president. Moments like that have a way of puffing up most people. That's why courage is such a vital part of a person's legacy. It supplies the grit to do the difficult.

Courage is the uncommon ability to resist when misguided instincts call for surrender. It's that tenacious resolve to do what is right, regardless of the pain. It requires a temperament willing to maintain convictions despite opposition.

When you stop to consider it, courage is a greater challenge in the little things than in the big. Although it takes unusual courage to die for something, it takes even greater courage to live for something. Dying for a right cause takes one right choice; living for a right cause requires hundreds of choices each day, day after day.

I don't think we lack parents with the courage to die for their children. Most would lay down their life without hesitation. What is painfully missing is parents with the courage to *live* for their children—to lay their self-interests, their reputations, and their discretionary time on the line each day. That takes uncommon courage.

We're Being Watched

Each day presents us with opportunities to teach our children about courage. We may develop great outlines and stirring lectures on faith, integrity, poise, discipline, and endurance, but if our kids don't see us courageously living out these character traits, they won't be inclined to pursue them.

Our children are watching. They're watching how we handle non-believing cynics. They're watching how we handle temptation. They're watching how we balance the competing demands of life. They're watching how consistent we are to the disciplines we preach. They're watching how well we stick with the things we started.

How we do in each of these areas will go a long way toward summing up the essence of our life. Our conduct is the legacy that will follow us. Our behavior is the legacy that will ultimately mark our children's character.

Emotional Courage

It takes courage to restrain our emotions from doing our thinking for us. If we let our feelings determine what we do, we can expect lives of consistent defeat. Loving parents resist the tugs on their emotions that incline them do what they *want* rather than what they *should*. We need courage to resist impulses. Without it, we surrender our families to the pain of debt and the frustration of distraction.

Our children's adult lives will be far more complicated than our own. They will need a kind of courage that stretches back into the formative years of childhood. Without it, they will be unable to resist the emotional demands of a depraved society.

Relational Courage

Life is a network of relationships. The people who crisscross our lives provide more than enough reasons why we need courage. Any relationship, regardless of how deep or how shallow, how weak or strong, how new or old, requires us to make courageous choices. What we do will tell our children everything about who we are.

It takes courage to take blame, to admit that we are wrong. It takes courage to swallow our pride, to fork down banquets of crow, and to submit to the consequences. The timid wimps of life stand and fight for their misguided pride and inexcusable actions. They pass the buck and make scapegoats of the innocent.

A courageous person faces those he has wronged and openly admits he let them down. When you admit you are wrong to your three-year-old boy, his eyes may fill with tears. But don't assume they are tears of shame. Far from it! They are tears of pride and confidence in a parent who is not afraid to face personal faults with courage.

When it comes to relationships, courage must work overtime. It takes courage . . .

. . . to be honest

. . . to love someone who has hurt you

. . . to forgive

. . . to confront someone who is wrong.

The Tests of Courage

A few weeks ago the battery went out on my car. Fortunately, I wasn't driving when it died. Unfortunately, my wife was.

She hitched a ride home with a friend and told me where I could find my unreliable car. I used her car to try a jumpstart. Nothing.

I hopped in the working car with my son in tow to make a pit stop at an auto parts store. I explained the symptoms to the man behind the counter. He felt certain that my battery had a bad cell and would need to be replaced. I figured he should know, so I bought a new battery. We finalized the sale and he explained the warranty. His statement went something like this . . .

". . . This battery is guaranteed for the life of your car. If it ever fails, regardless of where you are in America, simply take it and your receipt to any store that sells them, and they will give you a brand new one. However, the guarantee will be considered void if you have allowed the water levels within the battery to drop below the marked minimum. So, if you do forget to maintain the battery and it fails, make sure that you fill it with water before you take it in to the dealer. He would have no way of knowing that you had not maintained it properly and would be forced to honor the guarantee."

He said it with a matter-of-fact tone and a straight face. I took the battery, my receipt, and my son out to my wife's car and headed for the disabled one. On the way over I explained to Cody why the advice of the man at the store should not be followed. Psalm 15:4 says that a man of integrity "swears to his own hurt."

After I installed the new battery I had to take the old one back to the store to collect a five-dollar trade-in. My boy stood next to me as I horsed the heavy battery onto the counter. The same man waited on me. I asked him to check the battery to make sure it had a bad cell. He picked it up and carried it into the back room.

I suppose some customers have more the look of a fool than others. He apparently figured that somewhere along my life journey I had fallen out of the "Stupid" truck and it had backed over my head. I knew that the hand-held machine used to test batteries barely weighs a pound. I knew it would have been much easier to bring the tester out to the counter than to take the battery out back. I also knew I was dealing with a man of questionable character.

When he returned without my battery I wasn't the least bit surprised. He said it had a dead cell and was useless. I realized the chances were high that he was right, but I wanted to see with my *own eyes*.

When I told him what I wanted to do, he exploded. His rage was immediate, vocal, and threatening. My son stood next to me, and the shop was filled with customers. Everyone was staring at me and the man, wondering what I would do next.

Believe me when I say I don't get any satisfaction from moments like this. I'm not afraid of confrontation when all the muscle is in my corner, but this situation had me terrified. In similar, past situations I'd played the coward. But my boy was next to me and he'd have his share of these situations himself. So I held my ground.

It wasn't worth the five bucks, but it was worth the principle.

I reminded the clerk of the advice he had given when I bought my new battery—that I should be prepared to deliberately defraud the manufacturer. His attitude made it hard for me to place any confidence in *anything* he said. I wanted to see with my own eyes whether the battery was ruined or merely discharged.

In a huff he ran to the back room, retrieved my battery and the tester, brought them back out, slammed them down in front of me, clamped on the test cables, pushed the load button, and stuck the gage in front of my face. The battery was ruined.

I thanked him.

He wasn't amused. He popped open his cash register, slapped a five-dollar bill on the counter, and told me to get out of his store.

"Gladly," I said, as I took the money and my boy's hand and walked out. While strapping Cody in his car seat I noticed that most of those who had been in the store had walked out behind me.

It was an altogether unpleasant scene, but it had to be played out. Duty to my conscience and to my son took priority over my popularity with a dishonest businessman.

Moral Courage

Our morals are constantly tested. Our standards must be high and they must be maintained. But maintaining moral integrity can't be done without a courageous spirit.

It takes courage to tell the truth.

It takes courage to refuse to pass on gossip.

It takes courage to say no when everyone around you and everything within you is saying yes.

It takes courage to confront addictions—not just to drugs or alcohol, but to work, money, food, lust, pornography, whatever.

It takes courage to stay sexually pure in a culture that has gone crazy over sex. This world has marked our kids for moral annihilation. We need to prepare them to make courageous choices.

Two people immediately come to mind when I think about this. Jerry and Cheryl are parents of three beautiful daughters. Their girls have been the beneficiaries of a loving and stable spiritual environment. But even with all this godly teaching and understanding, with all this love and security, Jerry and Cheryl knew that without courage their daughters could easily fall to outside pressures.

Just about the time their oldest daughter, Shelly, blossomed into a beautiful young woman, they decided to do something memorable to help her maintain courage. It was easy for them to develop a plan because they knew what character traits they were trying to encourage.

They took some of their own gold jewelry, had the jeweler form it into a key, strung the key on a chain, and made it into a necklace. They washed their car, dry-cleaned Jerry's suit, and bought a simple corsage.

Then Jerry took his daughter out on her first "adult" date.

They enjoyed an elegant dinner in one of their town's finest restaurants. During the meal Jerry talked to Shelly about the courage she would need to stay morally pure. When dessert was served, Jerry took out the gift-wrapped jewelry box containing the necklace. But before she put it on, he told her its significance.

The gold symbolized her purity and the key symbolized the key to her heart. She was to wear it as a reminder of the moral purity that God wanted her to bring to her honeymoon bed. Every time she went out on a date, and anytime she might be tempted to compromise her purity, this gold key around her neck was to remind her of God's view of marriage. Then, on the night of her honeymoon, she could take it off and give it to her husband. With it she could let him know that she had preserved her purity as a gift for him.

Maybe that's why I like Jerry and Cheryl so much. They realize that courage doesn't come easy; but regardless of its cost, it must be transferred to their children.

Spiritual Courage

Our world doesn't take kindly to people who are unashamed of their faith. "You're free to believe whatever you want," the world seems to say, "so long as you keep it to yourself." Lay your faith on the table and you might as well lay it on the chopping block. When a culture worships itself, an individual who submits to God ruins everything. That's why faith is so valuable . . . and why it costs so much to maintain.

Frederick the Great didn't get his nickname because of a kind and generous nature. He was a powerful king who brutally crushed all opposition. His well-deserved reputation for fierceness was accompanied by his caustic cynicism toward God.

H. G. Von Zieten was one of Frederick's greatest generals. One day, at a gathering of military and royal dignitaries, the king told coarse jokes about Jesus Christ that had everyone rolling with laughter.

Everyone except Von Zieten.

Unable to remain neutral and with full knowledge of the potential consequences, Von Zieten rose stiffly to his feet and addressed the king.

"Sire, you know I have not feared death. I have fought and won thirty-eight battles for you. I am an old man; I shall soon have to go into the presence of One Greater than you, the mighty God who saved me from my sin, the Lord Jesus Christ whom you are blaspheming. I salute you, sire, as an old man who loves his Savior, on the edge of eternity."

The room went silent until Frederick the Great broke the quiet. With trembling voice he replied: "General Von Zieten, I beg your pardon! I beg your pardon! I beg your pardon!"

The crowd dispersed without a whisper.

No one can enjoy the treasure of an intimate relationship with Christ without paying a price in courage. Since our faith lays the foundation of a legacy of love, we must be prepared to pay any price for it.

One of the hardest things for anyone to do is admit his or her need for God. We are programmed to be self-sufficient, to throw our best up against life's worst, to be the captain of our own ship and the master of our own fate. It takes a courageous man to admit that he isn't as good as his motivational tapes tell him he is. It takes a courageous woman to realize that she can't get one-quarter of an inch closer to God on her own. It takes courage to humbly submit our lives to God.

Actions that Keep Us Courageous

Since courage is indispensable in the creation of a

loving and lasting legacy, we need to take the necessary steps to help it grow. Here are several:

1. Learn to confront your fears

The best place to start is to admit what frightens us. We need to acknowledge that we feel helpless, that we're afraid of the future, that we're not the parents we should be. There's nothing wrong with fear—unless we try to deny it.

2. Keep company with the courageous

One principle has repeated itself throughout my development of the six components of a legacy of love. It's this: Wisdom comes with righteous companionship.

The walk of faith is easier when we keep company with the faithful. The life of integrity is easier when the people who surround us ask the hard questions and don't wink at compromise. The poised and balanced life is easier when we congregate with people who have an enlightened sense of the appropriate. The disciplined life comes easier when we spend time with the disciplined. Endurance is easier when we run with people who know how to crash through walls of frustration and finish the race.

Courage is equally contagious.

Courageous people turn the timid and shy into giants of courage. We need to sprinkle our lives with regular and generous doses of fellowship with courageous people.

3. Never forget who's ultimately in control

At the beginning of this chapter I introduced three people who occupy prominent positions on our family "Wall of Fame." They aren't there just because of who they are or what they did. They are there because of *Whose* they are. My mom and dad and my friend Joe have taught me courage because they never lost sight of the One who controls their life. A few years back my mother went to enjoy the presence of the God she loved so much. Her legacy now lives on in the children for whom she spent her life.

Our children must be equally prepared. They are moving into a future full of cowards. The world in which they'll raise their families will be a world enamored with grandiose ideas of its own importance. It will preach the gospel of self and will seek out and destroy the weak and the anchorless. One of the greatest legacies we can leave our children is the legacy of a mother and father who love them enough to risk being courageous.

I want to close this chapter by taking you into the back chambers of Westminster Abbey. This ancient and majestic cathedral is the burial place of some of the greatest figures in England's glittering history. The crypts and monuments that crowd the walls and basements of this mighty structure pay tribute to the reputations and accomplishments of the people buried there.

One monument stands alone as a stunning and noble statement of the courageous man buried beneath it. It states his name, Lord Lawrence, the date of his death, and sums up the essence of his life in one single sentence:

"He feared man so little,

Because he feared God so much."

TEN WAYS TO TEACH YOUR CHILDREN COURAGE

1. Spend a day working at a rescue mission.

2. Read them James Clavell's brilliant short story *The Children's Story . . . But Not Just For Children* (don't tell them anything about it first) and then ask them questions about it. Don't worry, you'll know exactly what to ask them at the end!

3. Visit a fire department and ask one of the fire fighters to discuss courage.

4. Have a missionary over for dinner and ask him or her to talk to your children about courage.

5. Take a difficult stand in public (defending someone, political or social issue, religious issue) in front of your children and then talk with them afterward about what it is like.

6. Pick five courageous people (from the Bible, history, or your life) and discuss one each evening during dinner for a week. Have your kids tell why they think the person was or is courageous.

7. Take the kids to a nearby war memorial or military museum and discuss the courageous people who are depicted.

8. Teach them how to ride a bike, dive off a diving board, water or snow ski.

9. Have them talk to someone who was in a war.

10. Memorize Scripture on courage.

CHAPTER TEN

Designed
Dilemmas

I can't prove it, but I'm pretty sure that Satan invented the first shopping mall. All others since then are merely man-made modifications of the original.

Malls are to women what golf courses are to men. When you overhear your wife's phone conversation with a friend about their next trip to the mall, the conversation sounds similar to the one you had with one of your buddies last week about playing golf.

Do you want to shop Paradise Valley or Metro Center?

Do you want to play Orange Tree or Mummy Mountain?

Do you want to go to Diamonds and Sears, or do you have enough time to hit I. Magnin?

Nine holes or eighteen?

What are you wearing?

Are we going to stop by the clubhouse afterwards?

Are you bringing your Gold Card?

Are you going to try out your new graphites?

I've got to be careful on this subject because I'm aware of how sensitive some women get when men tease them about their shopping. The ladies know full well that although they do get a lot of joy out of shopping, they don't necessarily spend that much money. It's more like *therapy* than shopping. Besides, the real problem shopper in most families is the man. I like what Annie Chapman says about it: "Women go shopping all day, and they buy a blouse. A man goes shopping for two hours, and he buys a boat."

I had decided to play the back nine at our local mall one Saturday afternoon, and it made sense to Darcy that I should take Cody. Since I wasn't looking for anything in particular, it seemed like a good way to spend some time with my boy.

On the way over I was explaining to him how you play a round of shopping . . .

". . . You tee off from the West Entrance and play through J. C. Penney. Watch out for the bunker at B. Dalton, and be real careful coming out of K. G. Men's Store because you've got to put a mild fade on it to clear Goldwater's. They've got a lateral hazard just inside. If you land in there it's a two-stroke penalty plus you have to chip out with your American Express. . . ."

When we got out of the car, I could tell I had picked a bad day to bring a little kid to the mall. The parking lot was jammed, and people were swarming in and out of the main entrance.

I took Cody's hand.

As we got closer to the doors I explained that he'd have to hang on to me once we got inside. With all of the people it would be easy to get separated.

The mall we usually frequent is probably a lot like the mall where you shop. Straight through the doors on your right is McDonald's, Famous Amos, Chick-Fil-A, and a ten-screen movie theater. To the left is a large open area bordered by exotic eateries (for those with more discriminating taste buds), and then a large arcade for the teenagers. This is the nerve center of the mall, with everything else playing off it.

It was packed. Moving through the crowd made you sympathize with salmon. To complicate matters, there were several visual traps that could lure a little boy away from his dad. We had to stop to watch Ronald McDonald do some magic tricks, try out a few samples at the Chick-Fil-A table, and then get by the movie theater without staring too long at the posters advertising the latest Fifty-Ways-To-Meet-Your-Maker movie. I tugged a little harder to pull Cody away from the picture of Freddy Kruger on the latest *Nightmare on Elm Street* sequel, and mentioned that the hobby shop was coming up.

As soon as the words were out of my mouth he let go of my hand and bolted ahead of me. For a few seconds I lost him in the crowd. But then I saw my little blond guy weave through some shoppers and shopping bags to end up directly in front of the big window. By the time I got there he was kneeling down staring at the Lionel train that was moving just inches from his eyes.

I squatted down next to him and mentioned that I didn't want him running off like that. I pulled his chin over so that he had to look at me and said again that I wanted him to stick close.

"Right, Dad."

We looked at all the toys in the window for several minutes before going inside. The store aisles were thick with people, so I took his hand—for about five seconds. He saw a man demonstrating a remote control car toward the back of the store and sprinted ahead to check it out.

Once again I got his attention long enough to tell him to hang on to my hand. And once again his words acknowledged that he heard me . . . but everything else about him said he wanted to watch the car.

Back in the mall we walked about a hundred feet when he saw some children gathered around a lady reading a book.

In a second he was racing ahead of me to take a seat among the children. I stood in the background letting him take in the story to its end. When the kids started to disperse to their parents, Cody started looking for me. Once I called his name he came loping over, filled with animation about the story he just heard.

I let him finish before I told him *again* that he needed to stick with me. We had informed the children about mall kidnapings and about what to do if they ever got separated from us. But it was obvious from Cody's actions that he felt confident to be a carefree little boy and to let Dad worry about his safety.

I said earlier in the book that we have two responsibilities as overseers of our children. We have to protect them, but we also have to prepare them. I was more than willing to worry about Cody's safety, but somewhere along the way I had to prepare him to look out for himself.

We took a right to head down one of the main thoroughfares of the mall. Cody loosened his grip on my hand and eventually let go. He wandered in a big circle around me looking at the various displays in the windows. He wasn't the least concerned about sticking close. He wanted to run free. It wasn't safe for him to get so far away from me, but he just couldn't seem to see how important it was.

So I hid.

I slipped into the crowded racks of clothes at the entrance to Miller's Outpost. They provided perfect cover as well as an ideal vantage point to keep an eye on my boy. It bothered me how long it took him to realize I wasn't around. But when it struck him, the panic was immediate.

Instantly he started running in circles through the crowd, looking at every man who passed. His anxiety increased by the second. It was hard to hold back. Especially after the tears started flowing.

Nothing has quite the magnetic pull on parents' hearts as the helpless tears of their children. When you know that their whole world has crashed in on them, you want to pull them in close and shelter them from the hurt.

But he had only been crying about ten seconds. I felt pity for him, but few lessons are learned in ten seconds. So I let him experience the panic for a couple of minutes. It gave me time to formulate a plan for the follow-up to this lesson.

As soon as the lady with the big purse stopped to help him, I slipped out from behind the clothes racks and moved out into the mall where he could see me. He glanced up through his tears to say something to the lady when he suddenly saw me and charged over as fast as he could run. When he ran into my arms I was glad he was only three. If he'd been much bigger the impact would have sent us both flying across the parquet.

Our mall has groupings of benches in the middle of the thoroughfares. We holed up in one of these "islands in the stream" so that he could get composed and I could ask some questions. We reviewed what happened, what he felt, what he did, what he didn't do, and what he should have done. We talked about how it could have been prevented and also discussed a better plan of action if he ever found himself in that situation again.

That's called a *designed dilemma*.

It's creating a situation or an environment in which

children are forced to focus on their needs as well as draw conclusions about their lives.

Not the Way It Used to Be

A loving legacy must be transferred, not just given. It must be embraced and appropriated into the core of our children's hearts. We can't be satisfied with modeling (as important as that is). We must develop lessons for our children that compel them to wrestle (and therefore remember) critical truths.

The new look for the family makes this goal more difficult to attain. Age of Information families are too hurried, too over-scheduled, and too indulged. Such families lack the built in responsibilities that once made the teaching of character a daily part of childhood. Professional lawn services, prepared microwave dinners, maid services, and mechanized car washes take away some of the natural opportunities to learn responsibility. Our crowded schedules prompt many modern families to use paid outsiders to do what once were strictly family functions.

We don't even camp the way we used to. We've replaced tents, bedrolls, open fires, and hikes in the woods with Winnebagos equipped with kitchens, queen-size beds, VCRs, and dirt bikes.

I'm not against modern conveniences. When I live in the woods for a few days, I like to sit down to a tablecloth and Tom Brokaw, too. But the amenities often circumvent opportunities that build character.

I Never Want Them to Have It as Tough as I Did

Many families have encountered problems with their teenagers in the area of maintaining responsibility. Their kids have a selfish streak running down the middle of their character, and the parents can't get them to do anything about it. When you more closely inspect such a home, you see that few responsibilities have ever been imposed on the children, and by the time they become teenagers they have failed to internalize the character traits of work, commitment, and follow-through.

Their house may have:

. . . a beautiful yard they've never had to mow

. . . flower beds crowded with perennials they've never had to plant

. . . thick carpet they've never had to vacuum

. . . big windows they've never had to clean.

Their bedroom may have:

. . . soft linens they've never had to launder

. . . pastel walls they've never had to paint.

Their closets may have:

. . . comfortable shirts they've never had to iron

. . . tennis shoes they've never had to buy

. . . games and toys always picked up by someone else.

An outsider (such as myself) can make suggestions when the parents in these families run into problems with non-motivated teenagers.

"Um, do you think the problem might lie in the fact that your children are living in a five-star environment but don't have to do a thing to maintain it?"

That sort of line always brings out the excuses. One man told me that he didn't want his son (who was extremely irresponsible) to have to cut the grass, because he wanted to be able to take his kids to their beach house or mountain cabin whenever the urge came. If the son regularly had to cut the grass, it would impose constraints on the rest of the family.

Not everyone is as financially successful as this man. Most of us are glad to have *one* house to live in. But even the average family can be guilty of making life a little too easy. If you dare suggest to some parents that their child would do a little better if he had regular dilemmas that forced him to demonstrate responsibilities (like chores around the house or a part-time job), you may get a worn out rebuff. Like a skip on the album of excuses, there's one that keeps playing over and over again. As they sit in their perfect home, wearing their perfectly tailored clothes, they respond, *"I don't want my kids to have it as tough as I did."*

This is usually followed with stories about walking to school barefoot in the snow, having to work in order to pay for groceries, not having any money to go anywhere as a teenager, and on and on.

When I hear some guys tell these hard-luck stories of their childhood, I believe them. Yet in the back of my mind I say to myself, *How do you think you became so successful in your business?*

Part of the reason was that he *did* have it tough as a child. When life wasn't handed to him on the proverbial silver platter, he had to learn survival skills. Management skills. Coping skills. Unfortunately, that same man's desire to withhold discomfort from his children may turn out to be a curse rather than a blessing.

Lecture or Lab?

Who's kidding whom? We're not going to turn back the clocks. I, for one, don't want to. I don't want to go back to the days when we didn't know where tomorrow's meal was coming from. I like the security and the amenities that the modern living offers.

But we're relying too heavily on theory and lectures. We are quick to give our kids three-point outlines on faith, nail plaques to their wall with pithy principles about integrity, and tell them tear-jerking stories about courageous people. But life is more caught than taught. We don't appropriate until we've been forced to ingest.

We need to marry practice with theory and follow up lectures with laboratory experiences. That's where designed dilemmas play into the formula. Faith without practice is platitudes. Integrity is a lot easier to learn within the furnace of testing.

Suppose your child steals something from a store. There's a need for a lecture on honesty. There's even a need for punishment. But along with the lecture and the punishment, the child needs to take the item back to the store manager, make restitution, absorb the manager's anger, and maybe even spend some time talking to the policeman about it. I would much prefer my child learn a hard and embarrassing lesson about honesty now than get to adulthood with a streak of larceny that has never been checked.

Poise is a lot easier to develop when it is attached to dilemmas. Putting a child in a situation where he must choose between harsh or soft, trust or suspicion, passive or confrontive, forces him to practice the instruction he has received.

This concept has a biblical basis. Hebrews 5:8 makes an unusual statement about the Lord Jesus. It says, "He learned obedience from the things which He suffered." If you flip a few pages back in your Bible to Philippians 2:8, you can get a little insight into what that means. The Philippians passage says that from the human side, Christ had to submit to the heavenly mandate He came to earth to fulfill. Therefore, "He humbled Himself by becoming obedient to the point of death, even death on a cross."

In His younger years Jesus submitted to the sufferings that accompany the life of obedience so that He might be prepared for His greatest suffering, His death on the cross.

We can teach our children submission to God by creating situations that force them to appropriate the teachings we've given. Once they've seen our words make sense in real life, they are more inclined to make them part of the permanent fiber of their character.

When I took Cody to the mall, he was too preoccupied with glittery distractions to pay any attention to his personal safety. If that tendency isn't redirected, it can easily become a habit.

Without dilemmas pounding home the principles of character, a child has no way of knowing for certain that what we teach is true. Character-altering scenarios can do what our words never could.

Teaching dilemmas lie all around us. If we just use a little imagination and some personal discipline, we can use these situations as dress rehearsals for a lifetime of working through frustrating or puzzling predicaments.

I'll close this chapter with a list of some designed dilemmas you can use to build your child's character. But before I do, indulge me a moment of personal reflection.

As I think of my own childhood, I realize that my parents balanced my formative years with work and play. They taught me to delay gratification by not letting me play outside until my chores were done inside. With that principle ingrained in my personality, it was easier for me to apply the principle of delayed gratification to other vital areas of life. It helped me to understand the wisdom of turning my back on a promiscuous teenage life in order to have a fulfilling married life.

By having to spend time helping elderly people and babysitting little children, I regularly had to exercise poise, discipline, and endurance. Schoolwork, volunteer work, camping, fishing, participating in conversation at the dinner table, having to make it through the cold or to protect myself from the heat prepared me for the skills needed to stay married, help run a family, and survive.

Darcy came from a large family, too. She learned responsibilities as a little child. Her mother carefully prepared her for the responsibilities she would need to survive as an adult. She was groomed to respond properly to the demands of life both inside and outside the home. Her parents loved her enough to put her through the pain required to move potential into skill and promise into character.

Of course, we both have much to learn and discover. And with the best of training as children, we still have to struggle with pressures that may tempt us to take the easy route. But our lives as adults were made a lot easier through the dilemmas that our parents placed on our schedules to build for the future.

Booting Them Out of the Nest

When it comes time for our children to move out into the world of responsibility, they may find the world requires previous experience. Designed dilemmas will enable them to hold their head high at that first interview and know that they have what it takes.

• Being ready for school on time taught them the discipline of punctuality.

• Keeping their hair combed, their shoes shined, and their nails cleaned taught them that grooming can distract or compliment.

• Doing their homework every night taught them that tasks worth doing are tasks worth finishing.

• Taking care of their younger siblings taught them that forgiveness is necessary for peace.

• Practicing a musical instrument taught them that discipline can overcome a lack of natural skill.

• Submitting to curfews taught them that no one is without restrictions.

• Looking people in the eye, speaking clearly, standing up straight, and always using people's name with respect taught them that it's the little things that make a difference.

A legacy of love needs planned dilemmas to give it life. Our efforts on our children's behalf can save them from a world of hurt, and can allow them to enjoy the fruits of disciplined love for a lifetime.

TEN DESIGNED DILEMMAS
THAT DEVELOP CHARACTER

1. Spend Thanksgiving serving at a shelter for the homeless.

2. Arrange for your children to be given too much change at a store and see what they do.

3. Figure out what you're going to spend on each kid for Christmas and give them the option of having you use some of it to buy presents for needy families.

4. Set off the fire alarms, stand outside, and see how they respond.

5. For younger children, have them find your car in the parking lot at a mall, church, etc. For older kids, have them drive through rush hour traffic.

6. Have your children direct you home from a friend's house.

7. Take a family vacation to a poverty area (third world orphanage, reservation, etc.) and work the entire time side by side serving the people.

8. Give them an allowance and teach them how to live on a budget.

9. Get a pet and give them the responsibility of taking care of it.

10. Arrange for your child to be overcharged for an item and see if he or she takes a stand. Show your child how to handle it if he or she has difficulty.

CHAPTER ELEVEN

The Legacy of Your Marriage

At a breakfast sometime between our first night together and our first child, I announced to Darcy that I didn't feel very married.

It wasn't a threat. It wasn't a verdict. I'm not even sure I knew what I meant. It was just one of those observations that a person makes out loud and then realizes it was better left unsaid.

Now, don't get me wrong. Everything was going along on an even keel; we were mutually pleased with our goals and accomplishments. Nothing was amiss. I just didn't *feel* anything.

Darcy speaks tons with her eyes. And at that moment her eyes were telling me that I talk too much. In fact, for some seconds after I blurted out my silly announcement, her eyes did all the talking. She was studying me. Wondering. Thinking.

She stood up from the table, walked out of the breakfast room, and marched back through the house to her study (before you have children, you get to have a study). I could hear the drawer to her file cabinet open, then close.

She returned to the breakfast room, dropped our marriage license on the table, and made her own observation:

"You can *feel* any way you want. But this document says that you're married. And if you try to behave in an unmarried way, this document says that you'll regret it."

She was telling me what Jerry Reed, the country-western singer, said so perfectly a few years later: "I'll get the gold mine, you'll get the shaft." Although there wasn't much of a gold mine, I think she could have arranged for a fairly significant shaft.

My good wife knows that marriages aren't held together by feelings, but by promises. And promises kept are the greatest way to demonstrate to our children that we believe what we say about love.

Love grows through the struggles it endures. Our world takes issue with that. It doesn't think pain should accompany a heart filled with love. We want our marriages to read more like a Harlequin Romance, when too many of our lives read more like the *National Enquirer*. Things get tough. Spirits get testy. And the next thing you know, someone's pulling out the old Righteous Brothers album and singing "You've Lost That Lovin' Feelin'."

Because so many people approach marriage with misconceptions, they are shocked by its reality once they're inside. I heard it put this way: "Marriage is like a phone call in the middle of the night. First you get the ring, then you wake up." Far too many people, once they wake up, want out.

When you have an ordination certificate hanging on your wall, you occasionally are asked to perform a wedding. I can tell you first-hand that the best place to observe a wedding is about eighteen inches away from the participants. When you look into the bride and bridegroom's eyes and study them up close, you see past the anticipation and the nervousness. You can't help but look down the corridor of their future and wonder if these two people have a clue about what they're doing.

One anonymous man who apparently stood that close to many couples wrote his observations in a little vignette I spotted years ago. He captures the sense of how many pastors feel when they stand face to face with a couple about to be married. . . .

Assuming that sexual expression is irresistible, like a food, many couples inevitably find themselves standing before a minister to be married.

MINISTER: "Do you take this woman with all her immaturity, self-centeredness, nagging, tears, and tensions to be your wife—forever?"

The dumb ox, temporarily hypnotized by the prospect of being able to sleep with her every night mumbles, "I do."

Then the preacher asks the starry-eyed bride who is all of twenty, "Do you take this man with all of his lusts, moods, indifference, immaturity, and lack of discipline, to be your husband—forever?"

She thinks that "forever" means all of next week, because she has never experienced one month of tediousness, responsibility, or denial of her wishes, so she chirps, "I do," in the thought that now she has become a woman.

Then the patient minister parrots, "By the authority committed unto me as a minister of Christ, I pronounce you man and wife. . . . "

As he does he prays a silent prayer for forgiveness, for he knows he lies. They are not now husband and wife and he knows that few of them will ever be. They are now legally permitted to breed, fuss, spend each other's money and be held responsible for each other's bills. It is now legal for them to destroy each other, so long as they don't do it with a gun or club. And the minister goes home wondering if there isn't a more honest way to earn a living.[8]

You don't have to be the minister. Sometimes you feel it sitting in the crowd as you picture this young man and young woman facing the same battles that you faced:

I wonder if they know that the honeymoon feelings may not last through the honeymoon.

I wonder if they know that reality is immune to love.

I wonder if they know that the novelty of waking up next to each other wears off.

I wonder, I wonder, I wonder . . . .

But we bring our wedding gifts, we toast their happiness, and hope that their love will pass the test.

Sometimes it does. Too often it doesn't.

I don't think anybody captures the devastation of broken love quite like our friends in Nashville. When Willie, Waylon, and their fraternal order of tobacco-spittin' crooners pick up the plight of the broken heart, you never again look at the relationship between a man and a woman in quite the same way. I've been collecting lines from country-western songs for years. When they tell you that they aren't in love anymore, they're about as picturesque and honest as a person can get. I think you'll see what I mean.

One singer wailed of his irritation in the aftermath of a broken relationship . . .

. . . "She stole my heart, and now my suits fit funny."

Sometimes love fails because of a lack of advanced communication . . .

. . . "When she bleached her hair, it frosted me."

I sense that the man was a bit upset who sang . . .

. . . "Going from you to the gutter ain't up."

A gravelly-voiced singer asked a question that makes sense after a few days of contemplation . . .

. . . "How can I miss you, if you won't go away?"

One man offered to help you refrigerate your favorite . . .

. . . "If you want to keep your beer cold, put it next to my ex-wife's heart."

I'd rather not comment on this last one. I'll let the words speak for themselves . . .

. . . "I wouldn't take you to the dog fights, even if I thought you could win."

It's easy to laugh at love that buckles under real life pressures when it's being analyzed by a wickedly funny Nashville songwriter. But when you're in the middle of the conflict—when it's *your* heart that's being broken, *your* partner who's turned away, *your* children whose insecurity is being recorded on the permanent tape of their childhood—it's not funny.

I need to be honest with you here. I've been trying to slip in the back door of your conscience in order to say some hard things about the legacy of your marriage. I figured that if we laughed a little first, it could soften the blows that are coming.

Marriage is supposed to be the best example of love on earth. It's two people fused physically, spiritually, and emotionally, representing the ultimate illustration of the gift designed to sustain the generations. The most secure feeling a human being can experience is to be transparent with at least one other person within the safe harbor of love.

But the truth is that only a minority of marriages actually soar to the heights and explore the depths. Most accept a mediocre middle—and mediocrity spells the beginning of the end.

Let me quote for you a powerful description of lost love. When you get done reading it, ask yourself a question: "Is this an apt description of my marriage?" If your answer is no, you're not off the hook yet. You need to know that it could *become* so if you aren't careful. Here's the quote:

Their wedding picture mocks them from the table, these two whose minds no longer touched each other. They lived with such a heavy barricade between them that neither a battering ram of words nor artilleries of touch could break it down. Somewhere between the oldest child's first tooth and the youngest daughter's graduation they had lost each other. Throughout the years, each slowly unraveled the tangled ball of string called self. And as they tugged at stubborn knots, each hid his searching from the other.

Sometimes she cried at night and begged the whispering darkness to tell her who she was. He lay beside her unaware of her winter, for she warmed herself in self-pity. He climbed into a tomb called the office, wrapped his mind in a shroud of paper figures, and buried himself in customers.

And slowly the wall between them rose, cemented by a mortar of indifference. And one day, reaching out to touch each other, they found a barrier that they could not penetrate. And recoiling from the coldness of the stone, each retreated from the stranger on the other side. For when love dies, it is not in a moment of angry battle; it lies panting and exhausted, expiring at the bottom of a carefully built wall that it could not penetrate.[9]

Walls. Estranged love. The cold reality of life for thousands of moms and dads throughout our country. The winter freezes their joy.

Everybody wants good news. "Make me happy." "Don't spoil my day."

But there is no escaping the fact that our marriage is the single most effective tool we have for transferring a legacy of love to our children. It is also the single most powerful weapon for destroying the legacy.

Satan knows it. He knows that the future rests on the present. He knows that good marriages beget good marriages which beget good marriages. That's why he focuses so much attention on that aspect of our lives. He keeps firing at us. He knows that if our marriage crumbles, the legacy of love suffers . . . and may eventually disappear.

Everybody knows about our nation's epidemic of divorce. No one debates whether we have a serious problem. But what the experts have not been able to agree upon is how seriously the future will be damaged by the crumbling marriages of today.

Until recently the most outspoken voices have said that divorce has minimal long-term effects: "The kids get over it in due time." Some even wagered that a handful of kids came out of it better off.

That was until recently. One chilling study conducted over fifteen years has reported the effects of divorce on offspring. It said that many kids suffered serious problems immediately, while others fell in the category of "delayed stress syndrome." But the fact is that children who went through the trauma of divorce paid a heavy price in the decade-and-a-half that followed their parents' breakup. Nobody made it through unscathed—that's the critical point.

Marriage in the Land of Giants

You don't have to be a rocket scientist to see how this could be so. You simply have to be honest. Children who grow up watching their parents work through the frustrations of marriage are more likely to work through similar frustrations of their own.

Let me bring this home. What will happen ten or fifteen or twenty years from now when your kids . . .

. . . meet a giant called "bills"? If they have seen a working example of how a couple faces the pressures of unforeseen expenses or overdrawn accounts, they will know this giant can be beaten.

. . . meet a giant called "anger"? Will they remember how their parents always fought with the two-fold purpose of clarification and resolution, and recall that when the fight was over their parents were closer than when they began?

. . . meet a giant called "competition"? Will they remember that their parents had secured married love with cords of commitment, forcing their own wants and needs to submit to their vows?

. . . meet the giant of "boredom"? The best of marriages run into this one. When your children are married someday, they'll run into him, too. They need to have a courageous reference point. They need to be able to face the boredom of their marriage with the time-tested strategy gained from watching how their parents did the things necessary to bring excitement back into their relationship.

Whatever the giants, whatever the challenges, whatever the walls, our children need us to demonstrate that love is for real precisely because it perseveres over all obstacles.

Darcy and I could fall just as certainly as the next couple if we fail to pay the price of loving. When Darcy slapped the marriage certificate in front of me that morning years ago, she was just reminding me what the preacher said at our wedding. Our marriage was founded on a promise. I promised to take her for richer or for poorer, in sickness and in health, in good times and in bad times, and to keep myself only to her. She repeated the same vows to me.

So what if I get up one morning and don't *feel* very married? What difference does that make? I promised!

Fidelity to the promise is what makes our marriage a statement to our children about what love is and does. Therefore the promise becomes our legacy. We promise to love, we carry out that promise, and our marriage becomes proof positive of our love for our children—proof those kids can swear by.

That last statement is probably very painful for some of you. You're divorced or you were abandoned. Your partner left and took everything but the blame. There's no way you can change what has happened and your children have already internalized their impressions of you and of love. What can you do?

I wish I could say that God has a magic wand that He waves over your child's head, turning all the bad to good. But we all know differently. Leaving a legacy of love isn't a result of a series of fairy tale dreams and happily-ever-after endings.

The bad news is that the best we can work to do is minimize the impact of a marred love relationship.

The good news is that God's forgiving love can enable you to maximize the time you have left. He can touch the hearts of your children with a greater sense of understanding. He can help them to see beyond the pain of their parents' conflict and see the love underneath.

But it may require that you take some extremely painful and vulnerable steps. God needs to hear your prayers of remorse. Your children need to hear you admit that you let them down, that you are sorry, and that you need their forgiveness. Neither of these two steps can take place until you first forgive your spouse.

I know this sounds naive. Let's face it, you could catalog a long list of crimes against your heart. You could give hundreds, maybe thousands of reasons why your (ex)partner doesn't deserve to be forgiven. I'm sure I'd agree. But forgiveness isn't given because someone deserves it. It is offered as a gift in order to bring an end to bitterness.

When Christ hung on the tree in our place, He did it not because we deserved it but because He loved us. We can forgive, not from feelings of love for the person we are forgiving, but because of our love for Christ. Our honest forgiveness can preempt the buildup of bitterness in the hearts of our children, as well as in our own. It can give us the ability to transfer to our kids a sense of greater confidence in the love they'll need for the future.

(In the final chapter I'll deal more specifically with restoration of broken legacies.)

You may not be divorced. But it's possible the vignette I quoted about dying love just happens to describe your own marriage. If so, *it's not too late to do something about it.* The same principles that keep health in a good relationship can also be used to resuscitate a struggling one.

All of us want to instill in our children the character traits of love that will help them to thrive. I tried to put these traits into six easy-to-remember categories: Faith, Integrity, Poise, Discipline, Endurance, and Courage. Since our marriages are the most effective tools we have for transferring our legacy, and since marriage is the ultimate statement of what we mean by "love," we must be careful to monitor and maintain these same character traits in our relationship with our spouse.

These six traits form the perfect template for marriage. They touch our lives in the bedroom as well as the kitchen. They convict our actions as well as our thoughts. Husbands—you need to practice these habits with your wife (so do I). Wives—you need to practice these habits with your husband (so does Darcy). When we're faithful to this, we pass on a legacy that no one can take away.

The Habit of Faith

Faith is a muscle that requires regular exercise. No one has been granted the luxury of static faith. Faith either grows stronger or it grows weak and feeble. Strong and well-conditioned faith results from proper diet, proper exercise, and proper rest. Let's take apart each aspect.

The diet of faith

Faith thrives on a regular intake of God's Word. Sunday morning messages and small group Bible studies are the logical way to meet this need. But they aren't enough. We need fresh strength each day. That's why we must learn the discipline of daily Bible reading.

I'm not legalistic about *how*. I'm not legalistic about *when*. I'm just realistic. I'm realistic enough to know I can't expect my faith to be strong and vital if I deny it the food it needs. It needs the Word of God.

For years I played games with this subject. I began the Bible study habit only to end it. I did a lot of rationalizing about how busy my life was and how often I went to church and Bible studies. But all my rationalizations were lame.

At last I had to face myself and be honest. The truth was I had plenty of time for the things I felt were truly important. The only reason I could come up with for not faithfully reading the Bible was that I didn't think it was important enough. I had to admit that *God Himself* wasn't important enough. I also had to admit that my wife and my children's security were not important enough.

My kids' future is heavily influenced by my relationship with their mother. My marriage is heavily influenced by my relationship with God. My relationship with God is heavily influenced by the fellowship I enjoy with Him through His Word.

When I admitted this, I saw regular Bible reading in a different light. Instead of asking myself, "What's in it for me?" I began to recognize it as an investment in my relationship with the Lord, with Darcy, and with my kids. That changed my motivation and with it, my track record.

The exercise of faith

When I was in high school, I dreaded the last week of August. That's when I and forty other guys would assemble on the football practice fields behind Annapolis High School and stand before our football coach. We called him "Big Al." His nickname represented both the shadow that he cast and the strength of his leadership.

Big Al was a believer in many things. But the two things he emphasized most when we met in August were conditioning and conquest. He ran our tails into the ground so that when we entered our first game we would be prepared to win. He always held out those two items simultaneously. We always knew who our next opponent was—that kept us from walking away from the conditioning. But none of us would have kept with it if we didn't eventually get a chance to play somebody.

The Bible says Christians aren't wrestling with people, but with invisible forces of darkness. A marriage provides daily challenges to our spiritual lives. That's why we must exercise our faith if we want to strengthen it.

A husband and wife who use their relationship as an example of God's faithfulness, who reach out to those without Christ, are going to sense a strength of faith that will do wonders for improving their relationship with each other. When two people join hearts and hands with God to be a glowing example of His love, *they* are the major beneficiaries. But those little eyes and little hearts that watch their mom and dad benefit, too.

It's those little people who will someday form the next wave. Hand in hand with their spouses, they will lead the way of faith for the next generation.

The rest of faith

A healthy marriage needs time to ponder, reflect, and plan. So does a healthy relationship with God. Prayer is God's gift of rest to our faith. Through it we can praise, petition, and confess. It is this haven of rest that we need to habitually enter.

One of the ways we support our marriage is by specifically praying for our mates and for the children we are called to lead.

I like to pray when I run in the morning. It keeps my mind off how much I hate to run in the morning. When I pass my daughter's school, I like to pray for her, her teacher, her principal, and some of the classmates who wield so much influence in her life. As I jog through the needs of my family, there's a special word of help I like to ask on Darcy's behalf:

"God, give Darcy a great deal of fulfillment in her role as a mother today. Give her joy even in the mundane responsibilities necessary for meeting the needs of the family she loves. Help her to focus on the benefits of her immediate labors that provide a comfortable environment for love that lasts forever. Amen."

Praying for our partner provides relaxation for our spirit, our marriage, and our children. Combined with a regular diet of God's Word and the consistent challenges that come from reaching out to others, it will strengthen the faith we need to transfer a loving legacy to our kids.

The Habit of Integrity

Marriages don't last unless they embrace eternal convictions. At the top of those convictions must be commitments to the standards that protect love.

Love can't last if it is prostituted. If we feed our minds with pornography, maintain a circle of friends who value the friendship more than they do our marriage, or fail to guard the hidden recesses of our thoughts, we are going to find love difficult to maintain.

Integrity is a gift that we bestow on our spouse. Integrity boosts our mate's confidence in our relationship and provides a basis for trust.

The Habit of Poise

We need to practice the words and actions characteristic of two people in love. When a son gets married he should have no trouble knowing how to treat his wife. Why? Because he had watched his father treat his mother with public and private respect. Such a son will have a keen sense of timing based on years of observation.

Likewise, our daughters need to be shown how a wife maintains a loving relationship to her husband. A blend of easy pride and unencumbered devotion will flow naturally if she has witnessed her mother give a lifetime of love to her father.

The Habit of Discipline

Let me mention a few of the disciplines that nurture a loving relationship.

Speech

We need to guard our tongues from saying the cutting words that slice our mate's confidence. All of us occasionally fail in this discipline, and whenever we do we must be quick to reconcile. That means we admit we were wrong. If we cut her down in front of the children, then we seek her forgiveness in front of the children. If you slight him in the presence of the kids, then you apologize in the presence of the kids. At all times we should maintain the discipline of public and private verbal affirmation of love for our mate.

Sex

Two extremes in our sexual relationship must be avoided: *demanding* and *defrauding*. Sex is a gift as well as an expression. Its potential for selfish reward can sometimes encourage us to abuse it. We must avoid both the tendency to use it strictly for our own satisfaction and as a weapon to harm or control.

Physical

Gravity will ultimately win the war of the waistline, but that doesn't mean we should surrender. We lavish a gift on our mate and set a great example for our children when we maintain the disciplines of eating, exercising, and resting. Those disciplines, exercised according to our schedules and abilities, enable us to present to our family the healthiest and most attractive body possible.

Reading

In addition to our time in the Bible, we should maintain a regular program of reading. Newspapers give us the information we need to lead our family through sticky issues. Reading in wholesome areas of interest—fiction, biographies, hobbies—helps us to relax and provides needed release. It's also a good idea to maintain a regular reading list of Christian books on marriage, family, current issues, and our walk with God.

My wife helps me with that. Once I took off on a three-day business trip with luggage and briefcase in hand. I checked into a hotel room and opened my suitcase to unpack. On top of the folded clothing, dead center where it couldn't be missed, was a copy of James Dobson's book, *What Wives Wish Their Husbands Knew about Women.* I took the hint and had it read before I returned home. (Now if I can just practice its wisdom!)

Another book that would be a great investment in your marriage is *Building Your Mate's Self-Esteem* by Dennis and Barbara Rainey. Those are the kind of books that can be read once a year as a gift to your marriage.

The Habit of Courage

Courage is a habit. It gets easier and more natural with consistent practice. The legacy of your marriage will stand out in your children's minds as they remember the courage you brought to the commitment.

It takes a lot of courage to submit to one another, to put our partner's best interests ahead of our own.

It takes a lot of courage to work through conflict with the goal of resolution and reconciliation.

It takes a lot of courage to stand against the cultural attitudes that view marriage as tedious.

It takes a lot of courage to take the time to plot out the goals and objectives for your family that will allow you to leave a legacy of love.

It takes a lot of courage to stick with your strategy.

It takes a lot of courage to risk turning your back on influence, power, and money when those things undermine your commitment to the home.

It takes a lot of courage to be transparent—to submit your laughter, tears, hopes, and dreams to another person.

No marriage maintains faith, integrity, poise, discipline, or endurance unless it exercises large and regular amounts of courage.

The Habit of Endurance

I saved this trait for last because it's the one that enables our marriages and families to survive. A marriage that endures to the end has a better chance of producing children whose marriages endure to the end. In our twilight years, when the children's bedrooms are museums and the house is no longer filled with the sounds of little voices, we can enjoy the satisfaction of knowing we lived our lives for the glory of God's praise.

Some day one of us will have to say good-bye to the other. The pictures in the family album, the curios collected from a lifetime of travel, the empty kitchen, the empty chair, and the empty bed could haunt us. But if they are layered with memories of a life well lived and worth living, they could be the very things that comfort us through the hours of loneliness.

I'd like to close this chapter with a prayer for your marriage. It's made up of words and phrases I've picked up along the way that speak to the hearts of men and women who dare to live out their vows to the end.

A Prayer for Your Marriage

Father in Heaven, thank you for this husband and wife and their commitment to Christian marriage. As we look ahead, we pray that their future will never lack the convictions that make a marriage strong.

Bless this husband. Bless him as provider and protector. Sustain him in all the pressures that come with the task of stewarding a family. May his strength be his wife's boast and pride, and may he so live that his wife may find in him the haven for which the heart of a woman truly longs.

Bless this wife. Give her a tenderness that makes her great, a deep sense of understanding, and a strong faith in You. Give her that inner beauty of soul that never fades, that eternal youth that is found in holding fast to the things that never age. May she so live that her husband may be pleased to reverence her in the shrine of his heart.

Teach them that marriage is not living for each other. It is two people uniting and joining hands to serve You. Give them a great spiritual purpose in life. May they seek first Your kingdom and Your righteousness, knowing that You will sustain them through all of life's challenges.

May they minimize each other's weaknesses and be swift to praise and magnify each other's strengths so that they might view each other through a lover's kind and patient eyes. Give them a little something to forgive each day, that their love might learn to be long-suffering.

Bless them and develop their characters as they walk together with You. Give them enough hurts to keep them humane, enough failures to keep their hands clenched tightly in Yours, and enough of success to make them sure they walk with You throughout all of their life.

May they never take each other's love for granted but always experience that breathless wonder that exclaims, "Out of all this world, you have chosen me." Then, when life is done and the sun is setting, may they be found then as now, still hand in hand, still very proud, still thanking You for each other.

May they travel together as friends and lovers, brother and sister, husband and wife, father and mother, and as servants of Christ until He shall return or until that day when one shall lay the other into the arms of God. This we ask through Jesus Christ, the great lover of our souls. Amen.[10]

TWENTY-ONE WAYS TO LEAVE A LEGACY THROUGH YOUR MARRIAGE

1. Write a letter to your children on each of their birthdays, telling them why you value them. Present the collection of letters to them in a bound notebook on their thirtieth birthday.

2. Put together a "wall of fame," featuring pictures of key members of your children's heritage.

3. Do a study of your family tree and present it to each child when he or she is old enough to appreciate it.

4. Visit a key historical landmark at least once a year and tell how it played a vital part in their heritage.

5. Pray for the future of each member of your family every day.

6. Live below your means.

7. Get out of debt.

8. Create at least one dilemma per week for each child. Make it something that compels him or her to utilize principles that you've taught in order to get out of the dilemma.

9. Attend your child's parent/teacher meetings.

10. Pray for your child's teacher and principal every day.

11. Pray for the *parents* of your child's future spouse.

12. Write out a list of each child's greatest strengths and look for an opportunity to compliment her or him at least once a week.

13. Intentionally cancel important plans in order to spend time with each child.

14. Kiss and hug your spouse in front of your children on a regular basis.

15. Buy at least one heirloom-quality gift for each of your children each year (a quality picture, pocket knife, fishing lure, etc.) that he or she can save as a childhood memory.

16. Make a "Very Special Person" plate and feature each child twice a year. (She or he gets to sit at the place of honor at the table, pick the menu, and enjoy a central role in the table conversation.)

17. Make sure that you, as parents, are the first to explain the facts of life to your child.

18. Keep a daily journal of the key things that your children say and do. It will be invaluable when they are older. (This isn't as difficult as it sounds. Use an open block calendar. One or two sentences is all it takes to capture a day. My wife has done this for our three, and it's great to review their character development.)

19. Have a planning weekend once a year when you and your spouse get away from the kids in order to spend time planning out the *development of their character in the coming year* (I've included a "Legacy of Love Weekend Planner" in the appendix. It includes a preparation list, a weekend schedule, quiet time suggestions, and projects).

20. Have a planning weekend once a year when you and your spouse get away from the kids and spend time planning out the year to maximize the development of your marriage relationship. (I highly recommend Bill and Carolyn Wellon's "Marriage Weekend Planner." For information write to Fellowship Bible Church, 12601 Hinson Road, Little Rock, AR 72212.)

21. Attend a Christian marriage seminar at least once a year. (I recommend the Family Ministry Weekend, available throughout the country. Write or call Family Ministry, P. O. Box 23840, Little Rock, AR 72211-3840. Phone (501) 223-8663.)

Protecting the Legacy

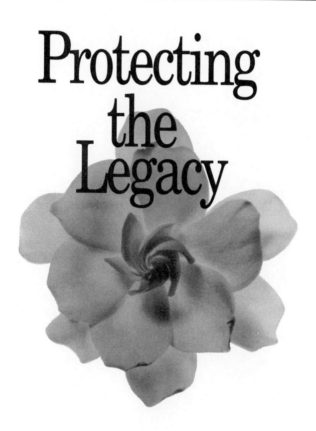

CHAPTER TWELVE

Emotional Latchkey Kids

One of the greatest contributors to conflict is bad timing.

I'd picked a bad time to call my wife, and I'd picked a bad time to give her a lecture about how hard I worked and how much I deserved preferential treatment.

My conversation with her from the Dallas/Fort Worth airport was seasoned with the typical macho-bread-winner statements.

"Who brings home the paycheck that he never gets to spend?"

"Who's the one who has to get up and get going whether he feels like it or not?"

Temporary folly from the mouth of a temporary fool!

I was on my way home from a conference where I had been speaking. My intentions were to call my wife to say hi and let her know my plans. But I happened to catch her in a "relevant" mood. When I told her I was going to go from the airport to my office to do some administrative work, she had the nerve to remind me that I'd been gone four days, that the kids were anxious to see me, that the administrative work could wait until the next morning, that I could rest on the plane, and that I needed to keep my priorities a little more in focus.

That's when I went into that foolish tirade about paychecks and getting up. I had not planned on her vetoing my agenda. I also had not planned on her seeing through my masquerade. The *real* reason I wanted to go to the office for the last three hours of my afternoon was because it was quiet. I could take my tired body and edgy emotions into the sanctuary of my work. By the time I'd get home, dinner would be on the table. We would eat. I could spend some token time with the children. Get them to bed early. And then I could crash.

But Darcy had different plans for me—like playing with the kids, talking to them, reading them books, and displaying exaggerated expressions of approval over all the art pieces they had worked on while I was gone. If I got home early, I'd have to work at being a father, and I had already been working to bring home the bacon.

My fatigue wanted to dictate my agenda, but my wife was motivated by balanced priorities. That's why she didn't budge from her position, nor did she pay any attention to my poorly timed words. She knew full well that although she did not work outside the home, she nonetheless made a significant financial contribution through the care she gave the family. She knew that she could write the book on "getting up and getting going whether she felt like it or not." She also knew that being an effective parent meant being inconvenienced.

The last thing I told her before I slammed down the phone was that I would see her at dinnertime and that she needed to be a little more sensitive to my needs. (That sounds like something *she* was supposed to say!)

I boarded the plane in a bad mood. My look of indifference declared to those around me that I wasn't interested in visiting on the trip back to Phoenix. They obliged.

It was somewhere over the bleak mountains of New Mexico that the captain first informed us that we had a problem.

His voice was all professional calm. (Pilots must go to school to learn to talk that way.) He assured us that everything was under control. But a blinking light in his cockpit indicated something wrong with the landing gear. He said he'd keep us informed. Great!

The banter that had filled the coach section of the plane began to subside.

A minute hadn't passed before he was back on the microphone giving us an update. He wasn't sure whether it was an actual hydraulic failure or simply a short in the indicator light. We would have to descend to a lower altitude and get in our landing pattern before he could actually try dropping the wheels to see if they worked. He again assured us that it was probably nothing and that everything would be all right.

Seats that had been in reclined positions started to slide back up.

The captain came back on with his FM disc jockey voice to let us know he had discussed our problem with the tower in Phoenix and that they would have emergency equipment standing by the runway.

Rosary beads started to appear in passengers' hands.

The cabin was now silent except for the whispers of flight attendants and the rattle of ice as they attempted to continue their beverage service as though nothing unusual was happening.

When a pilot switches on his microphone, you can hear a distinct but hushed static through the overhead speakers. Our captain turned on his microphone a couple of times like he was going to tell us something, only to turn it off. It added to the passengers' anxiety.

Up to this point I had not been too concerned. But as the tension of the people around me started to build, I found myself feeling more and more uneasy.

The captain came on again to let us know that he had personally tested the circuit breaker on the warning light and believed that it was functioning properly. That meant that the problem was in the landing gear.

Couples started holding hands. For all I knew, strangers were holding hands. The more our pilot discussed this "minor problem," the more dismal things looked. Now I was beginning to regret my conversation with Darcy.

Not wishing any of us to be in the dark, our captain came back on to explain how a problem like this is usually handled. He told us that we would pass by the tower so that the air traffic controllers could get a good look at our landing gear. If it looked like it was down and locked in place then we would attempt a normal landing. But because he wouldn't know if the brakes were working he would have to do a reverse thrust on the engines that would make the landing loud and awkward. If the gear wasn't down properly, then the crew in Phoenix would lubricate the runway and we would make a belly landing.

For some reason, he felt we would all relax if he told us the odds of each outcome. He said the problem was more likely with the brakes than the landing gear and that we would more than likely land with the wheels down. Then he assured us that if we landed with the landing gear in place there was only about a 30 percent chance we would be in any danger.

Wonderful! We're sitting in the back of the plane entrusting our lives to a pilot who gives odds like a bookie!

The silence in the plane was uncomfortable. A hundred people in an aluminum tube were flying somewhere over Arizona, and every one of them was thinking the same thoughts. We were certain that we were going to land in Phoenix. What we weren't certain about was just how far into Phoenix we would land.

The cockpit mike came on again. We braced for the worst. The captain was going to give us another announcement, and I figured it would have something to do with a limited supply of parachutes. But in his matter-of-fact way he simply said, "The weather in Phoenix is sunny with scattered clouds and a light breeze."

I'd been picturing me and debris all over the place, and this yahoo wants to give me a weather report!

We made the low pass by the tower, circled back for the landing, made a textbook approach, and landed without any real problems. It was a false alarm, but until we were safely on the ground we couldn't be sure.

The jolt of the 737's landing gear on the tarmac of Sky Harbor Airport shifted my brain from neutral to overdrive. I'd been vegetating in my aisle seat, preparing to accept my fate. The conference I had just conducted in Dallas, the argument with my wife, and the forty-five-minute verbal ordeal I had just endured at the hands of Mr. Microphone in the cockpit had left my brain feeling like a sponge after a three-day squeeze. But the shuffle of passengers gathering their carry-on baggage signaled a major transition.

It was time to return to the land of the living.

Cherish the Moment

I had made up my mind that if I landed safely in

Phoenix, I was *not* going to my office. The question mark that overshadowed my flight compelled me to reconsider my priorities. God had used my wife's wisdom and a blinking cockpit light to remind me that hours are gifts from God—and need to be invested wisely.

I walked off the plane with a reordered agenda. If I hurried, I could get to my neighborhood in time to pick up my daughter from school. I grabbed the first phone off the jetway to clear my plans with the home front (and eat a little humble pie at the same time).

Forty minutes later, I pulled my car into the string of family taxis that lined the curbs surrounding my daughter's school. A row of tired moms leaned heads against steering wheels, savoring a few moments of relaxation.

Five minutes before the last bell, my daughter's school exudes a quiet, academic charm. But looks have a way of deceiving. A churning restlessness boiled within its walls as hundreds of children tired of confinement were counting down the seconds to freedom.

At three o'clock this scholastic Mount St. Helens erupted. The doors exploded simultaneously, streaming rivers of kids across the campus in every direction. I got out of my car and took a position among a bunch of women in jogging suits. Because I didn't know what my daughter was wearing or how she fixed her hair that day, I was forced to study the face of every blond-haired kid that passed by.

Karis was one of the last ones out of the building. She emerged with an empty book bag draped around her wrist, her books and lunch box piled in her arms, and a sheaf of papers stuffed under her arm. She was talking at full throttle to a couple of friends when she saw me. She left them in mid-sentence and came racing down the sidewalk.

Her welcome was one of those unabashed Hollywood-type greetings where you drop everything you're holding and leap into a person's arms. She acted like I had just returned from a war.

And I cherished the moment.

I cherished it because she was young and her life centered around her family. It wouldn't always be that way. This little girl would soon be a teenager. Moments like the one that I was enjoying would ultimately give way to the crowded agenda of an adolescent girl moving away from her parent's sphere of influence. Capturing opportunities to go out of my way to communicate worth and value to her were essential.

As we were driving the three-quarters of a mile to our house we passed a kid from Karis's class walking home. My daughter mentioned that he didn't have a dad. His father had left his mother and moved out of state. This little boy was part of the growing statistic known as "latchkey" kids. He, along with one-third of the other school children his age, was going home to an empty house to await the arrival of a mother exhausted from work. He was a kid forced by circumstances to do a large chunk of childhood development on his own.

It made me appreciate the spontaneous opportunity to be with my daughter on a workday afternoon. I realized that she could be an emotional latchkey kid even without her parents going through the throes of divorce. Unless I determined to make my children a priority, we could go through life as strangers.

A child's best interests can become low priority even for the most well-intentioned parent. Battles with our own emotional and physical limitations make it difficult to keep priorities balanced.

Parents: Present but Unaccounted For

So far in this book we've looked at what a legacy of love is and how you can go about building one. Now I'd like to shift gears and suggest how to protect such a legacy—and what happens if we don't. The stakes are high, and we only play one round. What we do as parents has to count.

Many moms and dads leave their kids in the morning and head to work. They give their best ideas and the biggest share of their creative energies to their jobs. If we could read the back wall of their minds on the way home from work, we would see a grinding battle with fatigue. What these weary commuters wish for and what they know awaits them raises their frustration level.

Who *wouldn't* want to come home to a quiet house, soak in the bathtub for an hour, take a little nap, prepare and enjoy a leisurely dinner? But reality dictates terms as soon as the garage door goes up. The kids are there with their needs, their questions, their worries, and their secrets . . . and they expect us to give them our best. They can't understand that we gave our best to our employer and there's nothing left to squeeze out.

That's how children in good homes can end up emotional latchkey kids. Their parents are so preoccupied with their own personal needs and frustrations that they don't have time to focus on the emotional needs and frustrations of their children.

The little kids want to be held, the middle-sized kids want you to play with them, and the big kids want to be talked with rather than talked to. All of these activities engage their emotions and help to stabilize their fragile emotional systems.

When we parents succumb to our own needs at the expense of those of our kids, we force them to do the best they can on their own. Unfortunately, a child is not born with the intuitive skills needed to make balanced choices and draw right conclusions. Those skills are deposited in the early years by careful parents. If we are distracted from our duty we force them into a dangerous position . . . and leave them easy prey for the powers of darkness. They turn to their peers or their culture for emotional help—and it's like walking through a house of mirrors.

The Characteristics of Emotional Latchkey Kids

Kids left to nurture their emotions on their own start to show the wear and tear. Although there are always exceptions to the rule, observant parents can usually see the effects of the latchkey syndrome in their children. Kids go to one of two extremes: *unhealthy dependence* or *unhealthy independence.*

Granted, there are normal adjustments that come with the molding and development of a child's character that prompt temporary stages of over-dependence or over-independence. But we know problems are developing when an adjustment stage lingers long enough to become a life-style, when it moves beyond an extension of their personality to a layer of self-protection.

Unhealthy dependence

Some children demonstrate emotional latchkey tendencies through extreme fear and worry. They cry excessively, are overly reflective, and tend to cling to their parents when they are left behind. This isn't unusual for a child left in a nursery full of screaming kids, on the first day of kindergarten, or when being left with a baby-sitter he can't control. But when the child is older, facing normal, repetitive activities, and *still* can't muster enough independence to be on his or her own, it could signal a problem.

Unhealthy independence

Other children go to the opposite extreme. They protect their emotions through independence.

Sometimes their unhealthy independence disguises itself as maturity beyond their years. Their "adult confidence" may be a cover-up for a wounded ego. One way you can tell healthy independence from unhealthy is by how children respond to instruction. If their independence is really indifference, it shows itself in the child's frustration with instruction and leadership.

Many parents detect unhealthy independence through the consistent defiance of their child. It's like living in a constant cold war.

Open rebellion brings the quiet cold war to the surface. Battle lines are drawn and the child develops a show-no-mercy, take-no-prisoners attitude.

Overachievement, and the stress that accompanies the competition for first place, can be a telltale sign that a child is trying to protect his or her emotions. Excellence assures most children of approval from their parents.

Taking a Step Back

Sometimes the only difference between a routine and a rut is how they are spelled. Going through the motions of our daily responsibilities as parents can ease us into habits that take our children's needs for granted. Because most of us work hard enough to keep our bodies in a constant state of fatigue, we automatically look for shortcuts in child rearing.

Let me illustrate this by taking a look at the afternoon I brought my daughter home from school. For the record, Karis came home and practiced her piano lesson, watched a television program, ate dinner, did her homework (which included reading a short book), and finally went to bed.

If we step away from this scenario, we are better equipped to evaluate it. If you'll indulge me for a moment, I think you'll see a principle emerging from all of this.

My daughter walked out of a school operated according to an overriding curriculum, got into a car with an owner's manual in the glove box, came into a house that adhered to FHA specifications, sat down to a piano lesson tailored to her age and ability, watched a television show designed in a deliberate story-boarding session, ate a dinner prepared from carefully calculated recipes, and read a book written with the aid of a plotted outline.

The common link to all of these is a *plan.* The main parts of my daughter's day were the sum total of a series of predetermined options.

Leaving a legacy of love requires the same kind of forethought. A fulfilling childhood isn't the result of a chain of accidents and coincidences. It's a tapestry woven by the careful hands of loving parents who always have the "big picture" and the finished product in mind.

If we fail as parents, it is usually because we don't understand all that makes up the big picture. Children have three dimensions. They have a physical dimension, a spiritual dimension, and an abstract dimension that theologians like to refer to as the soul. This dimension is usually divided into the emotions, the intellect, and the will. None of these is a separate compartment. They are interdependent.

If we are going to fulfill our responsibilities to our children, we must have a strategy that takes all of these needs into consideration. Unfortunately, busy parents with complicated schedules don't have time to keep all of the needs before them in a balanced way. What we tend to do is concentrate on the dimensions that are easiest to measure—and easiest to delegate. The two parts of a child's makeup that get the most attention are the physical and the intellectual.

A quick peek down my daughter's afternoon schedule will show you what I mean:

School: primarily intellectual

Piano: At her present level, intellectual

Television: Intellectual (it was a nature show)

Dinner: Physical

Homework: Intellectual

Sleep: Physical

The interesting point is that the emotions were also involved at each level, but my wife and I had to make a choice whether or not to *involve ourselves* in them.

. . . We could drop her off and pick her up from school without ever having to personally monitor her progress and encourage her along the way.

. . . She could practice her piano lesson without any concerns for the esthetics of music or the benefits of disciplined work if we didn't come by occasionally, listen to her play, and let her know how much we enjoyed the music.

. . . We could let the television be her best friend, not bothering to investigate what her "best friend" has been telling her—or we could interact with her about the content of the programs.

. . . We could eat dinner with Vanna White and her "Wheel of Fortune" or we could take time to review the day together, exchange anecdotes, and pass on instruction.

. . . Her homework could be a tolerated evil or an opportunity for her parents to secure her intellect and hone her skills for the future.

. . . She could go to bed alone, or she could spend a few moments reviewing her day with one of her parents and planning out tomorrow. Some brief prayers and a kiss on the forehead could assure her of a safe environment in which to sleep.

Without our willingness to set our agendas around the inner needs of our children, those little ones could easily end up emotional latchkeys. This ultimately affects their spiritual confidence. If their intellectual and physical needs are our primary preoccupations as parents, we'll fail to notice when minor cracks appear.

A legacy of love demands that a conscientious parent oversee the various "programs" of a child in order to get the maximum mileage for a balanced childhood. And that's impossible if a parent isn't in position and involved at each level.

Unfortunately, the microchip generation of parents currently grooming the future has been taught that its primary focus should be on developing its children into highly skilled, healthy, superbly educated competitors. Christian parents also emphasize the spiritual. So we put our children in private schools, feed them natural foods, taxi them to dance classes, get them computer tutors, scream during their Little League games, make sure they're in Sunday school, and try to get them to bed at a decent hour. We score so high in these areas that we assume the kids are doing great.

But the real future of our children is wrapped up in how effectively they use their emotions and will to *balance* their physical, intellectual, and spiritual dimensions. It is the emotions and the will that must respond to the Holy Spirit, enabling spiritual principles to move to the level of life-style. They are also the tools needed to use intellectual information in a practical and marketable way. These tools must rule a body and force it into submission to a realistic regimen and schedule.

But tools aren't effective if the person using them is unskilled. For some children, the naivete and pre-occupations of their parents cost them their entire future.

It took a near belly-landing in Phoenix to remind me of that fact. I'm motivated to avoid another divine reminder.

CHAPTER THIRTEEN

Misguided Legacies

One summer my wife and I got an exotic opportunity to explore the outer islands of the Bahamas by sailboat. It was ten days of "Fantasy Island" as we snorkled the reefs and explored the isolated islands that dot the ocean around twenty-seven degrees latitude and seventy-seven degrees longitude. Boat repairs and a need for some supplies drew us into the harbor of Man-O-War Cay one afternoon. We decided to kill some time combing the outer beach. To do that we took a path that cut through the island foliage leading to the other side.

Just before we reached the beach, we stumbled onto a graveyard.

Standing among the tombstones, you could look across the tropical plants and flowers and watch the surf pound a white beach. What a view! If you had to be buried, this was about as good a place as any. What took us by surprise, however, were two open graves on the edge of the cemetery. Evidence of elapsed time suggested they had been dug many months earlier.

When we got back to the harbor, I met one of the island's pastors. In the course of our conversation I asked about the graves. His answer opened an interesting window into the way people on this island viewed life and death.

The island itself was a shallow hump of sand and vegetation on a coral platform. Digging a grave in the coral normally took several days. Since the island had limited refrigeration and no way to preserve a body until a grave could be dug, the government required that a couple of graves be kept ready for the next death. People were usually buried within hours of their last breath.

"But how do you assemble people in time for a funeral?" I asked.

His answer caught me unprepared. He said that they do the best they can for those who die suddenly, but if you happen to have a prolonged illness, they simply have your funeral *in advance.* Your family and friends carry you into the church or assemble in your house and have the funeral service with you there listening to it all.

When people tell me these kinds of things I have a bad habit of squinting one eye and looking at them sideways. It's the way I size up people who I think might be pulling my leg. He read my look and assured me that it wasn't as strange as it sounded. In most cases it worked rather well. It was especially nice if you got to hear a lot of great words about yourself. Unfortunately, he added, the people on this island were serious about their righteousness and had a reputation for brutal honesty. For some people, it added up to a bad news/bad news situation.

The bad news is, you're going to die. The other bad news is that you're going to have to hear what we think of your life before you check out. The cold truth could make you wish you were dead!

On a couple of occasions, however, the person who was supposed to die spoiled everything by *recovering*. Apparently attending your own funeral and hearing your eulogy in advance has a positive effect on those who live to tell about it. If good words are spoken over them, the reluctant corpses seem more inclined to keep up the good work. If they receive bad reviews at the funeral, they become motivated to change their lives for the better.

Tell me . . . what if your children got a chance to honestly eulogize you in advance? Right now. How would they characterize your life? What kind of words would they use? In what ways would the preoccupations of your waking moments have affected them?

Unless you get terminally sick on some remote Gulf Stream island, you'll probably never know the answers to those questions. But the thought *is* provoking. As I study my own life and the lives of people around me, I see legacies being built. Not all of these legacies are bad in themselves—only in the sense that they could easily become substitutes for a legacy of love.

Let's take a minute or two and look at some legitimate legacies that sometimes get out of hand.

A Legacy of Misguided Security

Security is the driving need to be safe. It's a God-given need that serves a vital function. It's the need for security that helps us win the battle of mind over mattress each morning. It inspires us to rev our inner engines and join the human rat race. It keeps us from letting ourselves completely cave in to the fatigue that the eight-to-five routine guarantees.

But sometimes our drive for security results from its unfortunate absence in our childhood. A vacuum in this compartment of our emotional structure compels us to elevate security from a need to an *obsession*. Security becomes the focus of our daily grind, overshadowing other needs of equal worth.

Since everything in the world has a price tag on it, it's understandable that many people assume money is the antidote to insecurity. The accumulation of money then moves beyond the simple need to finance life to become a quest . . . with security as its holy grail. The problem with using money as a hedge against insecurity is that it's so insecure itself! It tends to evaporate as quickly as it materializes. And its accumulation taxes our time like no other focus in life.

Love takes time, too . . . lots of it.

A legacy of love understands the need for a strong foundation of security in our family's life. It also recognizes the legitimate role that money plays. As long as money serves the divine interests of the family, it can be earned, accumulated, and spent without ensnaring us. It's when money moves from servant to master that we realize the true depth of our insecurities. And no child lives under the roof of a home controlled by money without being affected.

Henry Ward Beecher said, "No man can tell whether he is rich or poor by turning to his ledger. It is the heart that makes a man rich. He is rich according to what he is, not according to what he has."

A legacy of love demands risks. Sometimes we must jeopardize money's best interests in order to meet the highest needs of people. Children reared in a family that derives its security from money or the amenities it can provide are some of the most insecure people I've ever known.

A Legacy of Misguided Significance

Significance is the driving need to be recognized. It's the by-product of a creative God who made each one of us an original. It encourages us to do our best and allows us to derive personal value from our accomplishments.

But some people aren't satisfied with their God-given uniqueness. Something inside them longs for affirmation and applause. When better alternatives aren't offered, they run after the superficial status offered by society.

In this type of family, significance needs are not met by money as much as by the position money can buy in the eyes of peers. Keep in mind that we're talking about a legitimate need that gets out of control. There's nothing wrong with people thinking well of us. It's when we desperately need their accolades that we run into problems.

We're told that if you want something badly enough, you'll make the necessary sacrifices. But we need to ask honest questions about what or who is being sacrificed. Is what we are gaining worth what we are giving up?

Dennis Conner is outspoken on this subject. He's one of the most colorful and controversial yachtsmen in the history of the America's Cup. He successfully skippered the *Liberty* through all the preliminary races to earn the privilege of representing the New York Yacht Club in the 1983 cup challenge. The Royal Perth Yacht Club of Fremantle, Australia, sent its best to take on our best. This highly staged contest drew the world's attention in late summer of that year. Part of the excitement centered around the controversial winged keel of the *Australia II*. Conner and crew out-maneuvered the Aussie vessel to take a three-to-one lead going into the fifth race. But from there to the end of the competition, the race was all Australia. The America's Cup found a new home in Fremantle.

It was at this point that Conner, sailing for a new syndicate out of San Diego, set his sights on bringing the

Cup back to the United States. With a newly designed boat called the *Stars & Stripes,* Dennis began putting together his best team. As the man at the helm, he developed a boat and a team that brought a new standard of achievement to the America's Cup Race.

But when you get a closer look inside the heart of the man at the helm, you see a destructive craving for victory—and the affirmation that goes with it.

His quest for victory in The America's Cup (which he successfully won in 1987 by defeating *Kookaburra III* in Fremantle) is recorded in his autobiography, *Comeback.* His book outlines his personal thoughts about commitment. It's a telling indictment. But I'll let Conner speak for himself. . . .

> The three major factors to consider in a successful crewman are attitude, attitude, attitude. What we required of everyone was a total commitment to the commitment . . . everyone who made the team did so because they were prepared to dedicate themselves 100 percent to their job. I made it clear to everyone from the beginning that no one would make the team unless he or she put winning the Cup ahead of everything else in their lives: families, social lives, money, sex, religion, friendships. It had to be give all or nothing at all.

> I have a family of my own and I guess it could be argued that I have not been the best father or husband in the world. I chose, for better or worse, to commit myself to a particular goal. I'm not necessarily proud of that decision and it certainly isn't something everyone can make, but I made it and I expected everyone on *Stars & Stripes* to make it. Those who did not only survived, but flourished. Everyone on our boat was dedicated 100 percent to excellence, and I

believe that same dedication carries over into all of life as well.

My insistence on the commitment to the commitment has led me to believe I may be a bit abnormal and no doubt some people view me as insane. That doesn't bother me because inside I know how I feel, and I also know that if you're trying to take care of everybody else and to be Mr. Nice Guy and the world's greatest provider, the results will not be satisfactory. Part and parcel of the kind of commitment I demanded from the *Stars & Stripes* team was a certain kind of selfishness. Commitment to the commitment demands a very narrow focus. You have to start with a meaningful goal, something of the utmost importance, and then put everything else aside until you achieve that goal.[11]

That last sentence needs to be dissected. He said commitment requires a "meaningful goal." A meaningful goal has to be "something of the utmost importance." Everything else (families, social lives, religion, friendships) must submit to this goal.

The "meaningful goal" Conner set out to achieve is made of one hundred guineas' worth of Victorian silver—and it is only on loan. It comes with victory parades in San Diego and New York, a visit to the Oval Office, and numerous commercial endorsements. You also get your name listed in the sailing history books.

And the trade-off? Was the price paid for temporary stewardship of a silver cup worth the neglect of families?

Let me add a little footnote to all of this. Conner had to defend the cup against a New Zealand challenger a year later in San Diego. He christened a new *Stars & Stripes*. But instead of the single-hulled boats of the past, he sailed a catamaran. The new *Stars & Stripes* was lighter, faster, and more maneuverable than its competitor. It was no contest. Conner and crew won without effort.

But then, just a few weeks before I sat down to write this, a New York judge ruled that Dennis Conner's yacht club would have to relinquish the America's Cup and award it to New Zealand. Why? Because by racing in a catamaran they violated the "spirit" of the rules that govern The America's Cup. The judge called the race a "gross mismatch." (Like putting a dogsled up against a snowmobile). The San Diego syndicate will appeal the judge's decision. But regardless of the legal outcome, the record books will be forced to place an asterisk next to Conner's name.

"Commitment to the commitment."

"One hundred percent to your job."

"Put winning the Cup ahead of everything."

"If you're trying to take care of everybody else and to be Mr. Nice Guy and the world's greatest provider, the results will not be satisfactory."

By his own admission, Conner's legacy to his family may not be something desirable. But what is ironic in this whole scenario is that the real legacy he was trying to leave—being the greatest yachtsman in America's Cup history—may be tainted by the very ambition and drive for affirmation he felt was so vital.

Status. The need to be recognized. If it is misguided it could end up giving you the kind of permanent recognition that you never intended.

The kind of work I do occasionally gets me invited to be a guest on television shows. Interviews aren't the most exciting option in the TV guide, so the local stations do as much as they can to add zing to their programs. One of the best ways to liven up things is to add a studio audience. Unfortunately, live studio audiences aren't all that easy to assemble. Television runs on a bizarre time schedule. Many shows are taped at the worst time to attract a crowd.

But that doesn't matter, because television thrives on illusion. Need an audience? No problem. The technician in the sound room can add one at the touch of a button. The host introduces you and you walk in to enthusiastic applause. You say something clever and spontaneous laughter breaks out.

During a commercial break, I asked one of my hosts about the taped applause and laughter. He told me it was the standard track most shows use. Do you know how *old* that standard applause track is? They use recordings of people who clapped and laughed over forty years ago. Before I was born. That meant that many of the people I heard welcoming my entrance and collapsing over my jokes were not only absent from the studio, they were absent from planet Earth. I was being applauded by dead people.

Illusions on television are necessary and assumed. But it's sad when you watch people in real life driven to gain recognition from illusions fueled by a desire for status.

Our ego attachments to the plaques on the wall, the letters before or after our name, the write-ups in the society page, the name at the top of the letterhead, the photographs of us shaking hands with Who's Who types, and the strategic memberships to society's circle of elites send a damaging message to our children. It doesn't teach the superiority/inferiority of character, but the superiority/inferiority of *people*. If the child embraces this attitude as a crutch for his ego when he is an adult, he'll walk with an emotional limp for the rest of his life.

The legacy of status contradicts the essence of love. And since tomorrow's parents are living under our roofs today, we need to be serious about teaching a sense of significance that isn't fooled by artificial applause.

A Legacy of Misguided Strength

Strength is the driving need to be competent. It's that God-given desire to be very good at one thing and fairly good at everything else. With it comes a feeling of adequacy that keeps us from always looking over our shoulder at the competition. It's one of the great confidence-builders in life.

When the source of our strength comes from God, we can enjoy a sweet contentment. God's strength complements our personal strength and maximizes our ability to cope with constantly changing circumstances.

But the world is filled with parents who, for whatever reasons, have failed to appropriate daily strength from the Lord. Driven by fear, they take strength to volatile extremes. Their inability to cope with the unpredictable nuances of life leads them to exercise excessive controls. They flex their influential muscles too often.

Power brokers wield a lot of influence in the business arena. They get their faces splashed across the covers of the power periodicals and the tacky tabloids. Their autobiographies sell in the millions. They are obeyed because they sign the paychecks and they are respected because they hit the hardest. Being the Czar of New York or the Titan of Los Angeles or the Sultan of Scottsdale has advantages when you play the push-and-tug games of business. But bring those traits through the kitchen door and you've got a serious legacy problem on your hands.

Like all other dads and moms, abusers of power and control hand the future a new crop of parents. Unfortunately, these new parents are either too intimidated to assume the helm or too rebellious to steer a safe course. A legacy of love leverages strength in order to gain maximum benefit to the people it imprints. It understands that strength is merely *power under control.*

At this point you're probably feeling fairly safe. After all, those money, status, and power struggles are for the rich and famous. Right?

No. They are also the frustrations of the rank and file. They plague the struggling ghetto family just as much as the Bel Air family. That's because they are the misguided solutions the powers of darkness serve up to any ego regardless of race, creed, or net worth.

There's a simple reason why we choose to leave legacies of power, status, or money. They're easier to attain. A legacy of love requires a commitment of time, a willingness to work unrewarded, and a readiness to sacrifice personal agendas for the ultimate good of people who may not always acknowledge our efforts.

The natural resources of the world are napping in a crib down the hall and hanging off the top bar of the swing set in the backyard. They're in the kitchen leaving the lid off of the peanut butter jar and in the back bedroom playing the stereo too loudly. If you're a parent, you're in the process of mining and refining. Sure, you've got your own needs for security, significance, and strength, but you must be careful not to meet yours at the expense of theirs.

We can put our confidence in money, or see our money as a resource to leave a legacy of love. We can prop up our egos with status, or we can work to use our influence to achieve a safe tomorrow. We can play power games, or use love to impact others.

I've seen the urgency of this issue played out before my eyes again and again. My role as minister and counselor lets me peek under facades and gaze at the genuine hues of the heart. Sometimes rough exteriors give way in vulnerable moments. And there are no more vulnerable moments than in the presence of death.

Eulogy for a Stranger

It was a wet Christmas Eve in the desert, and this particular December 24th was sending a literal chill down the backs of our local chamber of commerce. They're the ones who coined the nickname "Valley of the Sun." An Alaskan front had dipped far enough down the weather map that Willard Scott felt compelled to inform America that Phoenix had a chill factor.

I had my Christmas Eve checklist ready and was on my way out the door when the phone rang. The distressed man's voice was unfamiliar. He said he needed my help. A twenty-two-year-old girl had died, a distant relative of his, and he was hoping I might have the time to perform her funeral.

My Christmas "to do" list was long. It didn't allow for time to stop and bury the dead. But I crumpled it up, stuffed it in my pocket, and assured the man I'd be there. Before I hung up I asked him to give me a couple details about the girl so I would know what to say at the service.

As he filled in the blanks I realized why a stranger was asking a stranger to bury a stranger. The girl was abused as a child. Molested by her father and beaten by her mother, she sustained deep emotional scars. Ultimately, she was abandoned. Orphanages and foster homes tried to help, but the girl's spirit was so disfigured that she spurned any attempt to care for her. Her home was a dumpster experience and she couldn't rise to see herself as much more than trash.

She hit the streets when she was twelve, survived by selling sex, and numbed her anguish with alcohol and drugs.

It was the drugs that finally got her.

A young girl. A brief, miserable life. An overdose. The man on the phone was a distant cousin. He had claimed the body in order to keep her from being buried in the potter's field.

I pulled up to the cemetery and stepped out of my car. A cold wind blew icy rain into my face. The man who had called me left his wife waiting by the casket and walked over to shake my hand. He apologized for the inconvenience. As I approached the casket it was obvious they'd purchased the "no frills" package. There was no mourners' tent, no chairs, no plastic grass covering the dirt. Just the casket, the cold, and a hole in the ground.

A man crouched next to a backhoe about a hundred feet away, smoking a cigarette. He was anxious for me to get on with whatever I was going to do so he could drop the casket, close the grave, and go home.

The plot was right next to a low fence that separated us from one of Scottsdale's busiest streets. This section of the cemetery was nicknamed "the cheap seats" by the salesmen at the mortuary. The quiet that should have accompanied this moment was drowned out by engines, brakes, and horns. The stranger handed me a photo of this girl as he futilely wiped rain from his face, a photo salvaged from her personal effects. Then he stepped back and huddled under an umbrella with his wife. That was my cue to begin.

The girl in the picture looked twice her actual age.

I fumbled to hang on to the picture, my Bible, and a little note card on which I had jotted a few useless words. Last minute shoppers, oblivious to the three people standing around the casket, raced by in their cars. I had to shout to be heard. In the few minutes we stood there, I tried to give some words that might comfort this couple's confusion and soothe some of their apparent guilt. I found myself distracted by the cold. The pages of my Bible were being ruined by the driving rain. I begged a merciful God to consider the circumstances, offered a brief prayer, and then everyone headed for their cars.

As I returned the photo to the man, his wife announced that the mall was going to close soon.

My car soon took its place in the Christmas Eve traffic, and I thought about the girl in the cheap seats. She lived alone, dreamed alone, suffered alone, and died alone. Her funeral was a small attempt at decency by a distant relative.

The thought that absorbed me the most was that the end of her young life was no accident. It was the logical conclusion of the legacy her parents had left her. If we could have seen a video of her childhood, we could have predicted her fate. But it was too late for blame. Just pity.

A Eulogy for a Friend

A few weeks after Christmas this year I was asked to do another funeral. But this time I wanted very much to participate in the farewell. It was a privilege to rearrange my schedule.

I had known Jerry for many years, and had been privy to the inner workings of his spirit. He had a wife, a son, and a daughter. Although he was a busy and successful man, he never lost sight of his purpose. He was a man who knew how to live, because he knew *why* he lived.

I'd like to close this chapter with portions of the eulogy I read at his funeral. It sums up a man who left a legacy of love. Please take the time to read these words carefully, remembering that someday, someone will be reading *your* legacy. What will it say?

> Tuesday evening, I gripped Jerry's hand, prayed with him, and slipped out of his hospital room. When I turned around to take one last look, he lifted an arm taped and jabbed with wires and needles and waved good-bye. The next day, he was gone.
>
> But in the sadness that accompanied his loss, I found a supernatural sense of hope. The hope was wrapped up in the essence of his life. Since

the news of his death, I've spent some quiet moments reflecting about him and what his life illustrated.

When I think of Jerry, three words come to mind. These three words are the sum total of a life well lived—and a life worth living.

The first word is *friend*.

Although most people claim to have friends or be a friend, few people understand the responsibility that comes with the title. Jerry was a welcome exception.

A good friend needs to be loyal. Jerry understood that a friend needs to know you will be there, regardless of the inconvenience. For those who were part of Jerry's network of friends, his faithful loyalty was an emotional oasis.

A good friend needs to be sensitive. I had occasion to be called upon as a minister to help meet some needs in Jerry's family. It was during those times I realized just how sensitive he could be. There were many times when I wondered who was ministering to whom. His concerns about me, my wife, and my children frequently caught me off guard. He seemed to have a keen instinct about other people's needs that made it a joy to be of help to him.

A good friend needs to be honest. What I found in Jerry was an ability to take honest words from a friend. That's probably what gave him the ability to give honest words when friendship required it.

A second word sums up Jerry's life. It's the word *family*.

Married to his high school sweetheart, Jerry was a

faithful and contented husband. They enjoyed life together. They accepted the reality that a good marriage is made up of both laughter and tears. Jerry was a good husband because he didn't get intoxicated by the good times or defeated by the bad.

(To his wife.) You and Jerry packed more fun into twenty-seven years than most marriages could ever hope for. All of those memories are locked safely in your heart. They are guarded from the fingers of death and nothing can steal them from you.

(To Jerry's children.) You are your dad's ultimate reflection. And you are also the best way that Jerry can remain a part of us. You are not only physical reminders of what Jerry looked like, but you can be emotional reminders as well.

Jerry was a superb memory-maker. And you have reams of family photo albums that document his flair for creating great events. When you look at those pictures, you can't miss that glint of pride in his eyes to be sharing a moment with the children he adored. Nor can you miss those demonstrations of affection from a father who loved you more than he loved himself.

He gave you values that could carry you through your adult life with dignity. You can thank him for your ability to work hard, your desire to treat people as inherently valuable, and your respect for the things in life that truly matter. Teamed with your mother, he gave you the ability to look people in the eye and to look at yourself in the mirror with confidence. He even gave you the option to walk away from him and his values without jeopardizing his love for you. He never let your mistakes or failures determine his pride in you.

That's because he wasn't tapping a limited well of perseverance, but an unlimited reservoir of love. His ability to be a good family man and friend came from the Power that propelled his life.

And that brings up a third word that captures the essence of Jerry's life: *faith*.

Jerry didn't just pledge allegiance to God, he loved Him. He knew that he drew his ultimate value from the God who was willing to pay the highest price for him. It was his confidence in the Lord Jesus Christ that gave him the ability to die with such dignity this past Wednesday. And you can be certain that the moment he took his last breath, his spirit slipped into the waiting arms of the God who loved him so much. A blood-stained cross and an empty tomb set Jerry free. Free to live, free to die, and free to live forever.

So let the truth of the cross help dab away your tears, and let the memories of a man who lived his life to the fullest comfort you when you start to miss him.

Your Eulogy

You are writing your own eulogy with every passing day. Today, as you read these words. Tonight, as you interact with your family. Tomorrow, as you move through your waking hours. Your words, your schedule, your choices, your obedience, the way you savor your victories and the way you swallow your defeats all help to define your life. It is this definition that your children rely on most as they seek to chart their own future.

Don't let any misguided legacies spoil the future for your children. Beware of the traps of misguided security, significance, and strength.

And be aware, too, that other false paths can detour the unwary from finding and enjoying a rich legacy of love. It's to those false paths—to counterfeit legacies—that we now turn.

CHAPTER FOURTEEN

Counterfeit Legacies

Traffic has a way of bringing out the worst in people. Just when you think you're starting to get your act together, God puts you in the backed-up lane to remind you that you haven't yet achieved maximum sanctification.

I had to be someplace in a hurry when I found myself creeping along a congested street. I was obeying one of Murphy's Laws by languishing in the one lane that wasn't moving normally. A swift line of unsympathetic drivers ignored my left turn signal.

It's situations like these that make seconds seem suspended in goo. I watched in my turning mirror for a saint, kept an eye on the homicidal driver in my rearview mirror, tried to keep from rear-ending the car ahead, all the while forming an opinion about the guy responsible for this.

There he was, about ten cars in front of me. He was driving one of those state-of-the-art recreational vehicles that has more whistles and bells than an F-16. He and his rig lumbered along, oblivious to the frustration they left in their wake.

A split-second lag in the lane to my left presented an opening. I seized it like a rush-hour bandit. A horn behind me saluted, and in a few seconds I was pulling past the RV. Up close I could see it was the best of the best. Somebody forked out a lot of money for all the amenities of this mobile condo.

At about eye level I spotted the bumper sticker. It explained one way to afford a rig like that. It said:

WE'RE SPENDING OUR CHILDREN'S INHERITANCE

I had to smile despite my frustration. Here were two senior citizens enjoying their twilight years in a high tech Winnebago. They'd worked hard, saved some money, and spent it in something they could live in while traveling the country. More power to them!

The sticker's message, however, hit me when I was organizing my thoughts about *Legacy of Love*. Although I judged the sticker was appropriate on the back of that RV, I couldn't help but think how accurate it would be stuck on the backs of many parents.

They've bought "The Lie" and are living "The Illusion." The Lie is that you can have it all without having to make major sacrifices. The Illusion is "Success." It's a deceptive life-style with superficial goals measured by relative standards.

Magazine racks are filled with periodicals whose very existence requires that The Lie and The Illusion be maintained. Supermom articles make balancing a career and a family sound like little more than a sophisticated juggling act—all you have to do is become a seasoned juggler. The problem is that keeping a career and a family aloft at the same time is like juggling Jell-o. It doesn't matter how skilled you get, a lot is still going to slip through your fingers.

Success seminars tell us to use hood ornaments and titles as yardsticks for measuring our true worth. They soothe our conscience by telling us all the wonderful things we can do for a family with the rewards that the success illusion offers.

While attending college, I spent my summer breaks on a variety of jobs. Most were in the construction field. One summer I worked as chief flunky on a bricklaying crew. I supplied grunt labor for the bricklayers and gofer services for the foreman.

I recall one particular morning when a middle-aged man and his son walked onto our job site looking for work. The man said he and his son hired on as a team but could hold their own on a crew. They looked hungry, and I would have hired them out of sympathy. But no one asked my opinion. The father had the tools of the trade and calloused hands as credentials. The foreman hired him and his son on a trial basis and assigned them to a foundation ready for walls.

We were building split-level ranch homes made of four-inch block with a brick facade. It usually took two men a full day to complete the eight-foot walls that made up the first story of the house. This man and his son, out to impress and anxious to win a position on the crew, finished the first story by the end of the first day.

The next morning the foreman asked me to install the metal frames for the doors and windows. I went to work, but nothing seemed to fit. I measured all the frames and they met the specs on the blueprint. But when I carried them into the house and tried them in the openings, they wouldn't clear the space. The bricklayer came over to see if he could help. I measured the window frame, and he measured the openings.

Based on our measurements, everything should fit. But still the frames wouldn't slide into place.

Finally the foreman came over to prod us along. I suggested that this particular house was being built in the Twilight Zone because nothing seemed to fit. When he stretched his tape measure across the openings, however, we discovered the problem.

I felt frustrated and sad as the foreman asked to see the bricklayer's ruler. He unfolded it and laid it on the floor. Then the foreman stretched out his own tape measure beside it and locked it open.

Amazing.

The difference wasn't much per inch—less than one-eighth—but stretched over the distance, it added up to an expensive blunder. None of the bricklayers knew it could happen. I didn't either. But it did—and it does. When quizzed about the ruler, the unfortunate man said he bought it from some "bargain barrel" at a hardware store.

He had bought a lie which made his speed as a bricklayer an illusion. In the end, the vital components of the home would not fit in their rightful place.

He was sincere . . . but wrong. He was skilled . . . but disgraced.

His work was a monument to a man who put his faith in an unreliable standard. After calculating the cost of getting custom windows and doors and a new set of prefabricated roofing trusses, it was decided the only way to fix the problem was to tear down the man's work and start over. I was embarrassed for him and his son as the foreman ridiculed them off of the job site.

Ready or Not . . .

We don't have the luxury of tearing down and starting over when it comes to our children. They're going to hit the future with a cry of "ready or not, here we are." We can't afford to squander their moral inheritance. As we deliberately build their lives, we've got to make sure that we build according to the proven standards of biblical truth that can weather the challenges of changing times.

Leaving a legacy isn't an option. We will all leave one—at work, with our friends, and with our families. The only choice we have is in the kind of legacy we leave. Most parents have good intentions. But we live in a world that serves up some uncomfortable nightmares. Nightmares like:

- stock market adjustments that radically deplete our net worth overnight
- leveraged buy-outs that remove our entire management team
- robots that eliminate the need for us on the assembly line
- financial demands that force both Mom and Dad into the work arena.

Add to any list the pressures of rearing kids in a media-oriented environment that can deprogram and reprogram our children's values faster than ever, and we find ourselves fighting a well-armed opponent.

That's why leaving a legacy of love is such a challenge. The parents with whom I work want to teach their children character traits that provide resilience against the negative challenges of the future. The problem is that the present stands in the way.

Whatever the reasons, we all bring certain negative characteristics to our marriage and family. It might be that the legacy inherited from our parents was highly flawed. It might be that we neglected good habits. It might be that we're trying to inappropriately satisfy inner needs of security, significance, and strength.

Regardless of the cause, the effect is the same—counterfeit legacies. They are the ill-timed words, the unfair actions, and the inappropriate motives that saddle the next generation with false notions of love and parenting. Our children are forced to lean heavily on these notions as they work their way through adulthood.

This chapter is called "Counterfeit Legacies." We leave counterfeit legacies when we tell our children we love them but our actions say something else. Counterfeit legacies leave kids confused about genuine love and handicapped as they move into adult relationships.

A Catalog of Counterfeit Legacies

A legacy of anger

Life behind the four walls of some homes is like living in an emotional mine field. Family members live on the edge, wondering when the next explosion is going to take place and how extensive the damage will be.

Several circumstances may feed this scenario—unemployment, graduate school, a prolonged illness, living in a badgered environment (i.e., too close to domineering in-laws, etc.). But these situations can be overcome.

The more serious problem is the family whose anger simmers just below the surface and which never seems to go away. Anger is a habit which glows like live embers in the corners of the soul. All an angry person needs is the right kindling, and the embers burst into flame.

Maybe it's the bitterness of an abused childhood, a forced marriage, an unfaithful partner, or circumstances that dashed some cherished hope.

A husband is angry because he never gets any breaks at work.

A wife is angry because she's not getting any help in rearing the children.

The children are angry because they never get any attention.

The list could go on and on. Regardless of the reasons, parents who fail to solve their anger are handing their children a bitter legacy. Inherited anger has the potential to slam doors of opportunity, decrease the invitations for deep relationships, and boil over into families of the future.

Anger is the by-product of life without relief.

Children reared in an angry environment suffer lives of emotional exhaustion. Punishment without relief is torture. Families who fail to deal with unresolved anger are sure to pass on their legacy to generation after generation—unless, of course, they receive a touch from the God of peace.

A legacy of fear

Fear is an enemy that usually gets the best of us through the little things in life. It's subtle. It slips in through the cracks of doubt and worry.

Let's draw a distinction here between healthy fear and unhealthy fear. There's nothing wrong with being afraid. If we are afraid to go down a dark alley, scale a cliff, or ford a strong stream, that very fear could save our lives. Fear helps us solve those dilemmas by forcing us to take the precautions necessary to keep us safe. But when fear paralyzes us and keeps us from doing the things that best serve our family, it harms the people we are called to love. When our fears are so great that we refuse . . .

- to confront
- to be honest
- to fulfill intimidating responsibilities
- to stand for our convictions
- to be transparent before our mate

. . . then we place our family in subtle bondage.

An interesting verse in 1 John 4 contrasts fear and love. It says:

There is no fear in love; but perfect love casts out fear (v. 18).

A legacy of fear encourages children to cower from doing the hard things that love requires. Love requires sacrifice, giving up a selfish insistence on personal rights. It means submitting your schedule to those you love and submitting your spirit to the God that bought you.

Love is expensive and takes risks. Fear isn't and doesn't. These two mix like vinegar and soda; they neutralize each other and leave a family bland. Fear takes the fight out of love. It kills that dimension of love that is willing to stand for what is best for others, regardless of the cost.

If perfect love casts out fear, then fear casts out perfect love.

Fear is the by-product of life without joy.

Children left with a legacy of fear are hamstrung when they move into adulthood. And the fear they've lived around may someday become the fear they'll live by.

A legacy of compromise

Some people spend their lives trying to get to their destination by shortcuts. They want the reward, but they don't want to pay the dues.

They want well-behaved kids, but they don't want the frustration that accompanies consistent discipline.

They want their kids to be good students, but they don't want to give up their evenings to help with math or science or English.

They want a strong marriage, but they don't want to go through the pain of resolving conflict.

They want integrity without putting forth the moral sweat it requires.

Compromisers are convinced they can play the game without following the rules. If life were the game of tennis, they'd want to get rid of the net because it keeps blocking their serve. They'd want to get rid of the lines because it's too difficult to stay inside them.

Compromisers lack a sense of calm and safety. They want to win without risking loss. People without boundaries and expectations are emotionally enslaved. They don't recognize that boundaries in life were designed to set them free.

Compromise is a by-product of life without freedom.

Children reared in compromising homes never seem to know when they're in-bounds or out-of-bounds, when they're safe or out, when they're found or lost. It's a legacy that yields frustration and sadness, and it can stalk us all the way to the grave.

A legacy of laziness

The main ingredient in the recipe for excellence is sweat. You don't get to stand on the top step of an Olympic platform because you're lucky. Luck wins lotteries, not Olympics. Name any noble accomplishment and you'll find a price tag of sacrifice attached to it. That's life. That's good.

But there are those on the sidelines with star qualities who never show up for practice. They've taken underachievement to new heights. They've watched the workout and don't want to put forth the effort—the sweat—required for success.

They're not immobilized because they are afraid of failing. That's a genuine fear, and it intimidates many people. Lazy people, however, aren't afraid of failing—*they're afraid of succeeding.*

It's sad to watch lazy people in the academic arena. They deliberately shut the door on knowledge because they know that once they walk in that door, they'll be forced to think.

It's sad to watch lazy people in the work arena. They deliberately shut the door on opportunity because they know that once they achieve, they'll be measured by a higher standard.

It's sad to watch lazy people in the family arena. They deliberately shut the door on responsibility because they know that once they start caring, they may have to love for a lifetime.

Maintaining a home requires on-going effort. The home is simply an illustration of life. For the children living in the home, it can serve as an excellent dress rehearsal for the future. But a legacy of laziness shuns commitment, responsibility, and follow-through.

Laziness is a by-product of life without discipline.

Children given a legacy of laziness grow up feeling guilty. They know they are turning their backs on their God-given potentials and God-given responsibilities. In the end they ache—they want to dream but they don't know how.

A legacy of legalism

It was hard to believe my eyes. On the television screen before me were two elementary school boys with oversized King James Bibles in their hands and chips on their shoulders. They screamed verses of condemnation and judgment at their principal, at teachers, and at fellow students. They didn't want converts but conquests. There was no love, just laws; no sensitivity, just dogma. In the background, just on the edge of the TV screen, stood the misguided parents who were encouraging this nonsense.

A nation watched along with me and shook its head in sadness. We all knew these little boys were merely parroting what they had learned at home. We also knew that if they kept this up through life, they would enslave their spirits to the legalism they urged on everyone else.

I'm willing to give such parents the benefit of the doubt; I assume their motives are sincere. They are no doubt convinced that they are doing what is best for their children. But the legacy of laws that they've forced upon their kids will counter the ultimate impact of love.

We've all seen examples of parents who stress certain boundaries to a destructive extreme. They use the rules of the Bible as weapons and take selfish pride in how well they are "obeyed." When parents' confidence is placed on the laws of Scripture rather than on the God of law, it's only a matter of time before those laws dig a pit for the emotional life of the people they are supposed to be leading. They make this mistake because they forget the condition of those who follow them.

Everyone was born with the same terminal illness—sin. A propensity toward doing wrong is innate at birth. We never have to teach children how to throw a tantrum, talk back, lie, or deceive. We do have to teach them to control their frustrations, show respect, tell the truth, and be open.

To keep our lives balanced we need laws to show us where we're safe and grace to draw us back when we drift outside the boundaries. Laws are maintained through discipline and grace is maintained through forgiveness.

Legalism is the by-product of life without grace.

Many children reared in this type of environment bolt from it at first opportunity. Unfortunately, they often run from legalism to unbridled license. Their unbalanced childhood over-shifts and they spend their adulthood living life at the extremes.

A legacy of intimidation

I could just as easily call this the legacy of control. It's a style of parenting that discourages individuality. And it comes from the heart of extremely insecure people.

You've seen as many of these types as I have. They rule with iron. They are not open to suggestions. It's their way or no way. The people around them exist only to accommodate their fragile ego.

What happens? Their leadership fails to draw out the best in their children and instead sends them cowering into corners. It's a sad, sad situation.

This need to dominate breaks every rule of leadership. Instead of helping a family to work as a team, such parents encourage anger, suspicion, and selfishness. Instead of enabling a wife to blossom and flourish, a husband relegates her to a bitter life of unfulfilled hopes. These are the Archie Bunkers of false Christianity. They yell, "Dingbat!" with a ball bat.

We typically picture the husband in this misguided role. But sometimes it is the wife, the mother, who is motivated by an overwhelming need to control.

Intimidation is a by-product of life without understanding.

It is the logical conclusion to a life that can't see past itself. And the saddest thing of all is that true leadership doesn't need to intimidate. Loving leadership moves people to action by quiet strength. It confronts rebellion with the strength of its position, its character, and its concern.

Parents who overwhelm their children drive them to bitter behavioral extremes. And the next generation pays the price.

A legacy of labels

It's not hard to spot people addicted to labels. And it's usually not hard to spot their kids. For example . . .

Dad bristles when people forget to mention his Ph.D. Mom insists on sitting at the VIP table. Dad is quick to mention that he has the corner office. Mom can't stand the thought that her best friend's house is in a more prestigious neighborhood than hers. Their list of friends is always seasoned with ego clarifications: "You know, the president of _____. The richest lady in _____. The most successful _____."

There's nothing wrong with having good taste or an eye for quality. Taste and quality can be the healthy result of refinement. But people preoccupied with labels are people who *need* symbols to complete their inner sense of sufficiency.

It doesn't take long before their children become preoccupied with symbols rather than substance. They derive their sense of value from what they are wearing and whom they are standing next to rather than from who they are and Whose they are.

The legacy of labels competes with the Holy Spirit. It quenches His work in the human heart.

Labels are the by-product of a life without confidence.

It is a legacy that leaves children empty, overwhelmed with doubts, and driven to achieve superficial goals.

A legacy of shadows

Success and achievement are wonderful results of work and utilized talent, and our media-oriented society makes notoriety and fame easy to attain. Whether by design or accident, the spotlight can beam down on a person overnight and allow the world to stare for a lifetime.

But some people prefer to stand in the shadows. Spouses and children may not be as excited about fame as the person standing in the footlights. They discover early on that the spotlight of fame is an X ray. It doesn't take long for the people who are studying us to see right through us.

Success and fame can breed terrific problems. Children are measured against an unfair set of standards. They must rise above certain behavior, be mature beyond their years. Sometimes they are expected to match the talent of their famous parent.

Ministers and preachers know this problem well. Their parishioners assume that if the pastor teaches on parenting, his children should be close to perfect. These misguided folks relate job security to how well the preacher runs his house. So for fear of being misjudged, pastors place unlivable demands on their children—which merely complicates the problem.

Fame can be a curse to a family. It can frustrate a parent's desire to leave a legacy of love.

A news story flashed over the radio and was followed up in the morning paper. The son of the famous Admiral Byrd was found dead in a Baltimore warehouse. His death revealed deep frustration and misery with being the son of someone famous. One article said he was never able to pull out of the shadow of his father. Admiral Byrd, enamored by the spotlight, never took the time to show his son how to cope.

Life in the shadows is a by-product of parenting without sensitivity.

We need to protect and to prepare. That requires us to understand the unique problems that our jobs or successes bring upon our children. With this knowledge we protect them, even if it means sacrificing personal fame or success. No personal glory is worth sending our children into adulthood unable to stand strong in the knowledge of their own personal worth.

A legacy of perfection

Living under the roof of a perfectionist is a lonely and bitter business. A child knows before he even tries that he won't do it well enough. Whatever it is, and no matter how hard he tries, he won't make the grade.

Children need affirmation. They need a sense of their parents' approval. That still leaves plenty of room for evaluation, critique, and high standards. But a perfectionist's standards are impossible. They can never be attained! Children reared in this type of home struggle with deeply ingrained feelings of inadequacy.

They *long* to be accepted by their parents. But Mom and Dad attach performance to their acceptance. Many children pursue straight A's, obtain highest honors, and excel at individual sports, for all the wrong reasons. Good goals for wrong reasons ultimately produce harmful results.

Too many children give up. Early on they see they can never meet their parents' approval, so they quit and save themselves a lot of work.

Perfection is a by-product of life without liberty.

Perfectionists are enslaved, and they're out to enslave everyone around them. Parents can easily be misled into embracing perfectionism as a life-style because it's so easy to confuse with the quest for excellence. It's an expensive mistake for which children must pay the rest of their lives.

A legacy of withdrawal

I'll let this next story do its own teaching. It appeared in an Ann Landers' column several years ago, but its truth is timeless. . . .

Dear Ann Landers:

I was moved to tears by a letter in your column from a mother who asked at what age a father and son should stop exchanging kisses and saying "I love you." Your reply in one word was "never"! How right you were.

A few weeks ago I kissed my son for the very first time and told him I loved him.

Unfortunately, he did not know it because he was dead.

He had shot himself.

The greatest regret of my life is that I kept my son at arm's length. I believed that it was unmanly for males to show affection for one another. I treated my son the way my father treated me. I realize now what a terrible mistake it was.

Please tell your readers who were raised by macho dads that it is cruel to withhold affection from their sons. I will never recover from my ignorance and stupidity.[12]

We can't give a legacy of love to our children if we deliberately withhold one of the greatest demonstrations of acceptance and approval—the righteous hugs, kisses, and "I love you's" from a parent who cares.

Withdrawal is the by-product of life without affection.

It tacitly punishes the innocent while protecting the misguided.

An unfinished legacy

Some of us start out with great intentions and even set enviable standards of love—but then pressures hit hard, defeat takes its toll, and commitment slowly gives way to convenience.

Maybe it's the dad who buys the theory that a mid-life crisis justifies quitting. Maybe it's the mom who looked too long at the grass across the fence and surrendered to the myth that problems go away when you walk out the door.

For whatever reason, some parents don't stay around long enough to finish the legacy of love they intended to give their children. They leave deliberately, unable or unwilling to cope with love's high demands.

An unfinished legacy is the by-product of a life without tenacity.

So many of these legacies are inherited. We're simply passing on what we received. It's like a multi-generational relay race. The baton handed to us might be inscribed with many different words: anger, compromise, laziness, fear, legalism, or love. We can't change the baton, but we can adjust the present and do something about the future.

This catalog of counterfeit legacies certainly isn't exhaustive. The pains and frustrations mankind has invented to pass on to his fellow man are myriad.

But the right kind of love can cut through all of this. It can overcome the past, figure out the present, and set a viable course for the future.

It isn't easy, but in the power of a gracious God, even a lost legacy can be recovered. In the next chapter, we'll find out how.

CHAPTER FIFTEEN

Restoring Your Legacy

Our frontline troops in World War II were supported by a well-organized and well-greased machine back home. The lend-lease programs that President Roosevelt had developed to support England and the Soviet Union started the machinery rolling, but it was when we actually committed our own young men and women to the hostilities that things really got moving.

One factory made brass casings for shells fired by tanks and large artillery guns. The calibrations had to be perfect and the brass had to be flawless. The workers knew that if they didn't do their jobs carefully, a shell could lose its accuracy or—even worse—detonate while being handled.

These munitions makers had enjoyed high production and flawless report cards from the front. But suddenly, on both sides of the ocean, word came back that crates of the casings were unacceptable and useless. The brass was corroded and flawed.

An investigation began immediately—*sabotage!* Everyone was assumed to be guilty until proven innocent. Someone was apparently coating the munitions with acid, and until the investigators figured out who, no one was spared the scrutiny.

Finally the saboteur was discovered. But it wasn't a person at all. It was an "it." *A peanut dispensing machine,* to be precise. During their breaks, the factory workers were getting salt on their gloves from eating peanuts . . . and the salt on the brass worked as a corrosive during shipment.

Unnoticed mistakes of the past had rendered useless a strong effort in the present.

Some of us know what that's like in regard to our home. We struggle to maintain the battle lines for the family in the present because we were sabotaged in the past. Incidents from our childhood cover us with emotional and spiritual corrosives. The list is endless:

- your parents beat you
- your dad was a workaholic and never had time for you
- your mother never praised your work
- your parents split up
- you were denied affection
- you were left alone most of the time
- your parents never told you they loved you
- you parents never disciplined you
- your parents made you perform for their friends; you were a sideshow for their ego
- you were sexually abused

- your parents never gave you any advice about money, work, sex, or marriage
- you were never allowed to tell your folks what was on your mind or your heart
- your parents never helped or encouraged you through school, sports, or hobbies.

You get the idea. Some kind of sabotage eroded your concept of love and handicapped you as you moved into adulthood.

Because you weren't taught responsibility, you have struggled with work.

Because you weren't given affection, you've had difficulty responding to your spouse and children.

Because you were never praised, you have fought huge battles with insecurity.

Because you weren't disciplined, you have a difficult time finishing the tasks before you.

Because of your bitterness toward your mother or father, you have punished those around you.

The problems of our past can hurt us in a thousand ways in the present. But somewhere along the way we have to stop the downward spiral of the "sins of the father." We have to put an end to legacies that have no business continuing.

Sandy Confronts a Lost Legacy

Sandy was a counselor at a family camp when Darcy and I first met her. Through the contact with our children, she and Darcy ended up spending large blocks of time together. As they became friends, Sandy began to open up about some of the pain in her past.

Reared by her mother and stepfather, Sandy's home had all the traditional appearances of a standard, suburban

American family. There were two brothers, one sister, a dog, two cats, and a gerbil. She remembered that her early years were filled with happiness. But two things happened that siphoned the joy out of her family.

It began the first afternoon her stepfather came home drunk from work. The family had seen him drinking heavily on an occasional Friday or Saturday night binge . . . but plastered at four in the afternoon? The problem was becoming serious.

His alcoholism slowly strangled the family. He would not only get drunk, he would get *angry* drunk. Terrorized by his violent rages, Sandy's mom and the kids started sleeping behind locked bedroom doors. Sandy remembers hiding under the bed after school to keep him from finding her.

The second serious problem occurred shortly after Sandy blossomed physically. The details aren't important. What is important was that her stepfather harassed her enough to create deep fear within her—and feelings of inadequacy about her womanhood. Although he never had sex with her, the damage was enough to take its toll.

All teenagers go through periods when they feel down or depressed. They need the comfort of someone who cares for them. Sandy's life was complicated by the fact that her stepfather took advantage of those times. He acted like he was trying to console her but would eventually demonstrate ulterior motives.

Throughout college and graduate school Sandy suffered from her stepfather's actions. She struggled through relationships with guys, kept them at a safe distance, and made it difficult for any of them to be a friend. She even showed unusual caution around her church friends. She went rigid if anyone (whether guy or girl) tried to give her a friendly hug. And she did what most people do to cope with a painful past.

She denied it.

I don't mean that she suppressed it, or acted like it never happened. She just *trivialized* it, refusing to acknowledge it for the major problem that it was.

But the awkward life and the deep insecurity finally got the best of her. She became convicted about her life through her study of the Bible. She knew that if she ever got married without dealing with this, her husband would feel the effects.

That's when she decided to take the courageous step to admit that the problem existed—that it had affected her in a negative way. She had to develop a plan to reconcile her past in order that she could once again enjoy her present . . . and recover hope for the future.

She did this by taking the problem to God. He, in turn, enabled her to forgive her stepdad.

It wasn't easy. It never is. But Sandy was helped by following some simple steps toward recovering her broken legacy. Let's walk through several of those steps to fix them in our own minds.

Admit that a Problem Exists

Like Sandy, you and I have to be willing to face up to our past and recognize there were things done at our expense that have hurt us in the present.

I'm not suggesting we indulge in excessive introspection or scour the corridors and closets of our memories looking for all of our parents' mistakes. Hey, there's plenty of 'em! After all, our moms and dads were humans who inherited their own sets of troubles.

It may be that your parents did a superb job of raising you. Some people, however, know without any doubt that they inherited certain destructive tendencies from their parents, and they need to honestly admit it. Without this painful first step, we can't come to grips with our past enough to alter its effect on our present.

Once we admit that our past was sabotaged, then we need to do something about the problems that have resulted in our lives. The second step, then, is to:

Take Action to Minimize Past Damage

I inherited a physical problem; I have the same kind of eyesight my parents had. Actually, I'm grateful, because they had fairly good vision. But in their late thirties they developed difficulty reading fine print. So did I. Almost on cue—just when I hit my late thirties—I started to develop bad headaches and itchy, red eyes when I did any prolonged reading.

I had a choice. I could submit to the inconvenience of glasses, or I could remain miserable. You're right! It would have been foolish for me to refuse something that could remove so much pain and help me see so much better.

In the same way, once we know there are things that can be done to relieve our emotional stresses, we should take the necessary steps. But I hear your arguments at this point. "Tim," you say, "getting fitted for glasses and dealing with a painful past are about as far apart as two things could be."

I realize that it takes a different kind of courage for you to face the past than it did for me to visit the optometrist. But the point still stands. If, by taking certain actions, you can get relief in the present—and thereby give your family some hope for the future—isn't it worth it? As I stated in an earlier book, "Love is the commitment of my will to your needs and best interests, *regardless of the cost.*"

So far, so good. Let's say you are honest enough with yourself to admit that your past has harmed your present.

Let's also say that you are willing to do something about it. What's the next step?

Reconcile the Past with the Present

You need a strategy that changes you on the inside enough to affect you on the outside. That's another way of saying "reconciliation."

I mentioned that Sandy forgave her stepfather. I don't mean to oversimplify a complex theological doctrine, but forgiveness has two sides to it. One side of forgiveness benefits the person who has offended us. It restores him or her to fellowship with us.

The second side to forgiveness is more self-serving (in a good way!). It frees *us* up to move on from the pain and preempts our bitterness.

Believe it or not, you can enjoy the second benefit of forgiveness even if you cannot arrange the first. You can uproot your bitterness and move on in your life even if the person who hurt you will not or cannot acknowledge his or her sin.

Let me explain.

Facts are facts. Some people will never acknowledge their responsibility for sins against you. Some people couldn't, even if they wanted to. They are on the other side of the world. They are feeble or frail. They are dead. It would be great if we could go back to our parents, explain to them the emotional pain they inflicted on us, tell them how it is hurting us in the present, and then listen to them take full responsibility. In most cases, however, that never happens.

But God gives us another option.

We can take our hurts to Him and leave them for *Him* to deal with. God is the judge. He is in charge of verdicts and punishment. By handing our pain to God we free ourselves to move on.

Some suggest that we should never forgive someone unless he or she first repents; otherwise, they say, we circumvent God's discipline. They may be right. But I also remember that Jesus looked down from the cross at the very people who gladly put Him there and said, "Father, forgive them; for they do not know what they are doing." Stephen, the first martyr for the cause of Christ, looked into the faces of those who hurled stones at him and asked God not to hold their sin against them (Acts 7:60).

Were the men who mercilessly crushed the life out of Stephen forgiven for their sin even though they hadn't repented? Scripture doesn't say. I believe they were still held responsible for their actions before God. But even if they weren't, each man had more than enough sin packed into his personal duffel bag to earn him a one-way trip to judgment.

Forgiving someone who has wronged us doesn't let that individual off the hook before God; it simply gives the person offering the forgiveness an avenue to deal with the pain and move on with life.

The Lord knew that He was dying for the very people whom He was forgiving. Because of His death, we can hand our anger to the God who forgave us and let Him decide what to do about the actions of those who hurt us.

Forgiveness is never deserved. It is a gift.

We may still have to confront our father or mother over their actions even as we ask God to take away our anger. But our anger can be placed at the foot of the cross, and the consequences for their sins and failures then becomes God's concern.

If we fail to do this, we'll have to deal with bitterness. And if we don't deal with bitterness, it will deal with us. Hebrews 12:15 highlights that point in bold italics.

> *See to it that no one misses the grace of God and that no bitter root grows up to cause trouble and defile many* (NIV).

Did you catch those last three words? . . . *and defile
many*. That's what our legacy can do if we don't do
something about the bitterness from our past. We end up
passing our anger down the line, and our children's
children can be victimized by the conflicts we refused to
reconcile with their great-grandparents.

As far as it is humanly possible, we need to resolve
our conflict with our parents. Personally. *Not* just through
the throne room of heaven—but personally. In words.

Without informing them of the conflict, we deprive
them of the opportunity to enjoy God's grace. And how do
you do this? I think the best approach is to begin by telling
them you love them. I know that's hard, but
remember—your children's legacy is at stake.

There is a song played on your teenager's rock 'n' roll
station that captures this point. Listen to the poetry of this
principle in the lyrics of the song, "The Living Years."

> Every generation
> Blames the one before
> And all of their frustrations
> Come beating on your door.
> I know that I'm a prisoner
> To all my father held so dear
> I know that I'm a hostage
> To all his hopes and fears
> I just wish I could have told him
> In the living years.
>
> Crumpled bits of paper
> Filled with imperfect thought
> Stilted conversations
> I'm afraid that's all we've got.
> You say you just don't see it
> He says it's perfect sense
> You just can't get agreement
> In this present tense

We all talk a different language
Talking in defence.

Say it loud, say it clear
You can listen as well as you hear
It's too late when we die
To admit we don't see eye to eye.

So we open up a quarrel
Between the present and the past
We only sacrifice the future
It's the bitterness that lasts.
So don't yield to the fortunes
You sometimes see as fate
It may have a new perspective
On a different day
And if you don't give up, and don't give in
You may just be OK.

Say it loud, say it clear
You can listen as well as you hear
It's too late when we die
To admit we don't see eye to eye.

I wasn't there that morning
When my father passed away
I didn't get to tell him
All the things I had to say.
I think I caught his spirit
Later that same year
I'm sure I heard his echo
In my baby's new born tears
I just wish I could have told him
In the living years.

Say it loud, say it clear
You can listen as well as you hear

It's too late when we die
To admit we don't see eye to eye.[13]

One of the greatest gifts we can give our children is a clean slate between us and our parents. We need to go back to our folks and let them know we love them. If we've taken the critical step of giving our bitterness to God, He will gladly give us the help to bridge the gap with our mom and dad.

One final step remains to resolving the past.

Take Action in the Present to Minimize Damage in the Future

Taking deliberate steps is the only way to ensure that the debris of our childhood doesn't damage future relationships. Here's an example.

Let's say that your parents never taught you manners. Maybe they didn't have any themselves. Regardless, you have paid the price for their negligence. The awkwardness that has dogged your steps has cost you romance, friendships, jobs, and some extremely embarrassing public blunders. What do you do?

First: You stop denying your past and admit that you have a problem.

Second: You commit to take action to minimize the damage sustained by your parents' neglect.

Third: You forgive your parents before God, and then (if they are alive) try to build a healthy relationship with them—starting with a declaration of your love for them.

Fourth: You start reading about appropriate behavior, make yourself vulnerable to a tutor, and move in to situations you once avoided in order to courageously face your problem.

This doesn't sound too hard when you're talking about a problem of poise. But if you're working through child abuse, molestation, alcohol, or problems of that nature, it's much tougher. One thing, however, is certain: If you do nothing, you're going to harm the people you love.

Is It Ever Too Late?

It may be that you're on the other side of this equation. It may be that you're saying to yourself, "Hey, it would have been nice if you had mentioned all this to me fifteen years ago. But the divorce (or the rage or the withdrawal or the legalism or whatever) has already taken its toll on our children."

My friend, nothing is going to go away overnight. Your children will have to make their own choices about what to do with the childhood that molded them. But you can help.

You can take responsibility for your actions and ask your children to forgive you. It won't change the past, but it will radically improve their future. By taking personal responsibility for your mistakes, you take the burden of guilt and anger off of their shoulders.

Let me slip back to the story of Sandy for a second. Sandy has gone through all the steps within her power to deal with her past—including writing her stepfather and telling him that she forgives him. He has not said one word to her about it.

But what if her stepfather had come to her and said something like this:

"Sandy, I said things to you and did things to you during your teenage years which utterly shame me. I don't blame the alcohol, or the circumstances of my life, or anyone but ME. You did not deserve that kind of treatment from me, but you've been forced to suffer because of it. I don't deserve your forgiveness, yet I want to ask it anyway. You are a wonderful woman who deserves a better chance, and although I cannot change what happened, I can do something about your future by removing any guilt or shame you might feel. Regardless of whether you choose to forgive me, I want you to know that I care about you, I'm proud of you, and I want you to experience the best."

I know Sandy well enough to know that if her stepfather made a confession like that, she would release him from his shame without hesitation. But the fact is, he hasn't said anything. Not a word. Certainly not an apology. That's hard on Sandy, but it doesn't change her resolve. Because she has handed God the problem, she is still able to hold out the prospect of reconciliation with the one who hurt her.

Are you?

Or maybe you're the one who's inflicted the hurt. You are the one who needs a pardon. Are you willing to step out and ask those you've hurt for their forgiveness?

I said it wouldn't be easy . . . but love reaches out regardless of the cost. We may need to go to our children and release them from any guilt that they may feel for a divorce. We especially need to do this if we used them as pawns or tools to get back at our "ex."

The process of reconciliation is hard. But it can be done, and there are scores of examples to prove it. I'd like to take a little time right now to mention three such instances in the Bible—three examples of people who allowed God to intervene in bad family situations. Each was handed a legacy of hate, a legacy of evil, a legacy of rejection . . . and yet each passed on to his children a legacy of love and faith. How did they do it? Let's drop in on their lives and see.

Joseph

Joseph is the best known of this trio. Every kid who has ever gone to Sunday school knows about him. His father, Jacob, indulged him, gave him preferential treatment, and esteemed him higher than his brothers. Naturally, the brothers got jealous. And before he knew it, Joseph was stripped, thrown in a well, sold into slavery and booted into Egypt. Once there, things improved as he became house manager for a wealthy Egyptian named Potiphar. But when Potiphar's lusty wife approached Joseph for some undercover work and he refused, he found himself framed and sent to jail. After *two years* in cold storage, Joseph earned a chance to solve a major problem for Pharaoh and was elevated to second-in-command over all Egypt.

All this had given him a lot of years to think about what his brothers had done to him and about how his father's unwise actions had triggered it all.

So when a famine brought his brothers to Egypt decades after they had wounded him, Joseph was in a position to make them squirm—or worse. He could have savored his revenge and let them absorb the full force of his anger.

But Joseph loved God and understood the laws of legacy. He wanted no part of a generational decline of his family.

He chose instead to allow God's forgiveness to heal the past and give hope for the future. Listen to what he said to his brothers as they stood trembling before this now-powerful man:

> Don't be afraid. Am I in the place of God? You intended to harm me, but God intended it for good to accomplish what is now being done, the saving of many lives. So then, don't be afraid. I will provide for you and your children (Genesis 50:19-21, NIV).

Interesting. Twice he tells them to stop being afraid. Once he tells them that God could use even their evil deeds to bring about good. And then the text adds this comment: "He reassured them and spoke kindly to them."

Joseph was ready to forgive when the opportunity arose. He hadn't sat around all those desolate years plotting revenge against his wicked brothers. How do I know that? Simple. Long before his brothers reappeared on the scene, Joseph became a father. And what he named his two sons speaks truckloads about what was going on in his heart. But let's allow the Bible to tell it:

> Before the years of famine came, two sons were born to Joseph by Asenath daughter of Potiphera, priest of On. Joseph named his firstborn Manasseh and said, "It is because God has made me forget all my trouble and all my father's household." The second son he named Ephraim and said, "It is because God has made me fruitful in the land of my suffering" (Genesis 41:50-52, NIV).

Manasseh: "God has made me forget." And Ephraim: "Twice fruitful." You don't get the impression Joseph spent too much time indulging his bitterness, do you? He grieved over his losses, picked himself up with God's help, and determined to give his sons the legacy of love he had been denied.

There's a touching scene recorded in Genesis 48 as Joseph's father lies on his deathbed. Joseph is summoned and brings his two boys. Now, he could have arrived at his dad's bedside full of resentment and anger. He could have punished Jacob for his past foolishness and negligence by denying him the comfort of his grandkids. But, as we said, Joseph understood the laws of legacy. He knew that unless the bitterness stopped, he'd pass on a heritage of rage. That's why he sat his sons on their grandpa's lap to receive his blessing. And that's how generations to come were blessed with Jacob's tender words:

> May the God before whom my fathers
>   Abraham and Isaac walked,
> the God who has been my shepherd
>   all my life to this day,

the Angel who has delivered me
    from all harm
    —may he bless these boys.
May they be called by my name
    and the names of my fathers
        Abraham and Isaac,
and may they increase greatly
    upon the earth
(Genesis 48:15-16, NIV).

Preserving a family from generation to generation.
That's what can happen if we let God have His way in our
lives. We can let Him take a pathetic childhood and turn it
into an avenue for His glory and our benefit. Like He did
for Josiah.

Josiah

When you talk about people with rotten family
legacies, Josiah has to be near the top of the list. His
grandfather, Mannaseh, took evil to all-time lows. He
rebuilt pagan altars that his father had destroyed. He
worshiped foreign gods, the sun, moon, and stars, and put
detestable idols in Solomon's temple. He organized
seances and contacted the dead. He practiced sorcery and
divination. He even sacrificed one of his own sons in a
firepit. His portfolio well qualified him for the top spot in
the ancient *Guinness Book of World Records* under the
heading, "World's Vilest Father." In fact, he *did* earn such a
title—but not in *Guinness*. Here is what the Bible says of
him: "He did much evil in the eyes of the LORD,
provoking him to anger . . . [He did] more evil than the
Amorites who preceded him" (2 Kings 21:6, 11, NIV).

Unfortunately, Josiah's father, Amon, was a chip off
the old blob. The story gets pretty tiresome:

Amon was twenty-two years old when he
became king, and he reigned in Jerusalem two

years . . . He did evil in the eyes of the LORD, as his father Manasseh had done. He walked in all the ways of his father; he worshiped the idols his father had worshiped, and bowed down to them. He forsook the LORD, the God of his fathers, and did not walk in the way of the LORD (2 Kings 21:19-22, NIV).

You may have noticed Amon reigned for only two years. Why only two? His officials murdered him, and were murdered in turn. And with that happy family history, Josiah became king.

With such a set of circumstances, who wouldn't predict a destiny for Josiah as dismal as his father's and grandfather's? But our God doesn't *predict* the future, he *makes* it. With his help, Josiah became one of the godliest kings in Israel's history. He broke the pattern of evil and wickedness set by his forebears and earned a reputation light-years from theirs: "He did what was right in the eyes of the LORD and walked in all the ways of his father David, not turning aside to the right or to the left . . . Neither before nor after Josiah was there a king like him who turned to the LORD as he did—with all his heart and with all his soul and with all his strength" (2 Kings 22:2; 23:25, NIV).

What an epitaph to grace your tombstone! Born into a family with a heritage of evil and idolatry unmatched in Hebrew history, Josiah made a choice to turn it all around by following the Lord.

You can do that, too. You can do it in the same way Josiah did—by turning to the Lord with all your heart and with all your soul and with all your strength. It's a life-changing step. And it's the necessary step which Jephthah took.

Jephthah

Jephthah may not be one of the most famous people in the Bible, but he holds a position of honor . . . even though he didn't at first. At least, not in his brother's eyes.

Let me explain.

Jephthah was the result of a one-night fling with a prostitute. His half-brothers pronounced him unworthy of the family name or of any of the family inheritance and disowned him.

He left the family disgraced.

He wandered to a place called Tob and settled there. "Worthless fellows" (the NASB's term) gathered around him and became his friends. Chuck Swindoll says of this group, "Had they ridden motorcycles, their black leather jackets could have read 'The Tob Mob' as they raced over the hills, outrunning the law of the land."[14]

Years passed and Israel's enemies grew strong. Battles went badly for the Jews and many Hebrew lives were lost. Their leaders grew frightened. What could they do? Then someone stood up and said, "I know what to do! Why not invite Jephthah to come back and lead us? He might be the son of a whore, but he knows how to fight. What do we have to lose?"

The leaders agreed and begged Jephthah to return. "Come," they said, "be our commander, so we can fight the Ammonites" (Judges 11:6, NIV).

Now, Jephthah could have allowed the past to sour him on the present. He could have laughed his family to scorn, spit in their faces, and sent them whimpering away. But he chose instead to protect the very people who had rejected him so cruelly.

Jephthah *did* return. He *did* fight for his family. He *did* become their leader. Oh, yes. And one more thing.

God placed his name in the believer's "Hall of Fame" found in Hebrews 11. Right there in verse 32, along with bigger names like Samson and David and Samuel and the prophets, you see it: Jephthah.

If this man—illegitimate, the son of a prostitute, disinherited by his family—could overcome those odds and wind up in the Hall of Faith, don't you think God might be able to pull off a few miracles in *your* life? If a man like Jephthah could reconcile with his brothers and sisters and then pass on to his own children a legacy of love . . . might it not be possible for you, too?

I know it is. With God's help, it's do-able. But you've got to try.

Guarding the Legacy

We can do several things to leave our children a loving legacy. A few, like Bible study, prayer, involvement at church, and service, almost go without saying. But let me list a few more that might prove helpful.

Mentors

All of us need someone who will scrutinize our lives and hold us accountable to the goals that keep our families on target. We need mentors, those significant folk who ask us the hard questions and refuse to back off when they get unsatisfactory answers. These are the men and women who love us enough to risk confrontation for the sake of our children.

Two couples serve that role for Darcy and me. We are "mutual mentors." I pray regularly for their children and they do the same for mine. We meet regularly to keep each other on track in our marriages and in our responsibilities as parents.

Small groups

Small groups are different from mentors. Every parent can benefit from a weekly accountability group, especially if it spends its time studying and discussing principles for maintaining a godly home.

Marriage conferences

Every couple needs to get away at least once a year to focus on their relationship. But couples need more than just a weekend away from the children. They need to go to a conference that has a curriculum and qualified teachers who present godly principles on marriage. These are vital to healthy marriages.

The Family Ministry out of Little Rock, Arkansas, has the best marriage weekend we've ever experienced. It sponsors conferences throughout the United States. For information on conferences in your area write:

The Family Ministry
P. O. Box 23840
Little Rock, AR 72211-3840

Weekly dates with your spouse

Any flame burns hotter if you fan it. A prioritized marriage sets aside time to keep the lines of communication strong. Schedule a night when you and your spouse can get away from the kids to enjoy each other's company. It's a superb example for the kids and will give them a deep sense of security, knowing that your relationship is going strong.

Monthly dates with your kids

Loving legacies aren't passed down without investing large amounts of time in our kids. We need to make appointments with them to do things individually. Dads don't "date" their sons, but why not ask your boy to join you at "The Breakfast Club"? That's what Cody and I do.

A legacy of love weekend planning session

We discussed in an earlier chapter the importance of having a blueprint for our children's character. To make that easier, Darcy and I set aside time each year to retreat as a couple to a quiet place and work on a strategy for our kids' lives. We concentrate on their long-term needs as well as on immediate ways of moving them toward the six major character traits.

To make this easier for you, I have included in the appendix of this book a weekend planner for building your child's character.

Prayer

Earlier I said prayer was a "given," but I think it deserves special mention. One of our greatest acts of love for our children is to lift them before God each day. To pray for their hopes, fears, habits, struggles, friends, and teachers requires a working knowledge of their daily lives.

Pray with your kids. Pray with them at mealtime and at bedtime. It's a lot easier for a child to slip off into dreamland when the last thing he or she remembers is a mom or dad kneeling next to them praying for their safety.

Let me mention one more option for prayer. Darcy and I have started praying for the *parents* of the children who will grow up to marry our children. We figure that they will have the most influence on those who will join with our kids to form the next generation. I don't know who they are, but I know the God who does. That's why I like to pray on their behalf. By the way, I pray that those parents will be instilling the six characteristics of love into *their* children—therefore, I pray that they will develop them in their own life.

It's Never Too Early

Whether you are single, engaged, newlyweds, expecting, or just got your first bun from the oven, it's never too early to begin the process of developing a lifestyle that spells l-o-v-e. Character requires commitment regardless of age or status.

All of us can make big investments in our community by being the kind of people who create righteous heritages for the little folks we touch.

It's Never Too Late

When we get a glimpse of an ideal, then take an honest look at our tangled lives, it's only natural to moan, "What's the use?" Undoing years of frustration seems like an insurmountable job.

Of one thing I'm convinced: With God, it is never too late. Regardless of the depth of pain or the size of the chasm stretching between the members of your family, God is ready to wrap you in His arms and walk with you through whatever agony might be required to restore your legacy.

I know how trite that might sound. And I know it's easier for me to write those words than it is for you to live them out. But trust me, please. God *is* there, He *does* care, and He *will* walk with you on the painful road ahead. How do I know He will? Because He demonstrated His unbending commitment to you on the cross. And that will never change.

Holding Firm No Matter What

The days of Judah were numbered. The people had grown so evil that God had no choice but to deal decisively with their sin. The Babylonian siege of Jerusalem began during the ministry of Jeremiah the prophet, and before it was over most of the Jews would die.

Right in the middle of it all, stuck between Jeremiah's prophecies of doom, lies a refreshing story of faith. God calls Jeremiah to contact a family hiding in the safety of the city. Recabites, they're called. They were one of the few families in all Israel who had remained true to the Lord and to His commands.

God commanded Jeremiah to speak to the families of Jerusalem and to use the Recabites as a godly example.

They had obeyed the advice of their forefather when he advised his children to avoid doing business with the Israelites, to avoid living among them, and to avoid their bad habits. I love how this story ends. Let's pick it up in Jeremiah chapter 35.

> Therefore, this is what the LORD God Almighty, the God of Israel, says: "Listen! I am going to bring on Judah and on everyone living in Jerusalem every disaster I pronounced against them. I spoke to them, but they did not listen; I called to them, but they did not answer."

> Then Jeremiah said to the family of the Recabites, "This is what the LORD Almighty, the God of Israel, says: 'You have obeyed the command of your forefather Jonadab and have followed all his instructions and have done everything he ordered.' Therefore, this is what the LORD Almighty . . . says: 'Jonadab son of Recab will never fail to have a man to serve me' " (35:17-19, NIV).

A righteous display of godly character—a legacy of love—preserved this obscure group of nomads from feeling the heat of God's wrath. The obedience of one generation laid a foundation for the blessing of generations to come.

None of us knows what is waiting for our families in the future. But we can be certain that a proper legacy will secure good things for years to come.

In 1944, General Douglas MacArthur was honored as "Father of the Year" not just for his leadership as a father figure to a nation at war, but because of his deep affection and leadership of his only son. I think his speech is a fitting conclusion to this chapter on restoring a lost legacy:

> By profession I am a soldier and take pride in that fact. But I am prouder—infinitely prouder—to be a father. A soldier destroys in order to build; the father only builds, never destroys. The one has

the potentiality of death; the other embodies creation and life. And while the hordes of death are mighty, the battalions of life are mightier still. It is my hope that my son, when I am gone, will remember me not from the battle but in the home repeating with him our simple daily prayer, "Our Father, Who art in Heaven . . . ."[15]

Lost legacies *can* be recovered. It will take work, sweat, time, and determination. But most of all, it will take the ingredient that General MacArthur knew so well: "Our Father . . . in Heaven."

Epilogue

Before we head our separate directions, there's one last little side trip I'd like you to take with me.

Stand with me on a small patch of ground in a cemetery just outside of New Castle, Pennsylvania. It's not that big, and it's not that impressive, but I like to come here every once in a while. It's a good reminder.

The main reason I can find this small plot amidst all these tombstones is because my grandfather placed a five-foot monument right in the center. He had it put here long before I was born. We buried him a couple of years ago, just behind it.

Five generations of Kimmels are represented here. It begins with my great-great-grandfather, Jacob. He was born in 1836 and emigrated from Germany with my great-

great-grandmother Louisa. She was three years younger than he. He worked in a nuts and bolts factory that was torn down about a hundred years ago. She was a homemaker but ran a little candy business out of a front room of their house.

Like all immigrants, they had to watch their money closely. She was the bookkeeper of the family and allowed her husband fifteen cents a week for spending money. They saved everything they made in the candy business. That's what they used to buy an entire commercial block in their town. That established them adequately enough for Jacob to get a little more spending money. Louisa died of pneumonia in 1901, he of a stroke in 1905.

Next to them is my great-grandfather Fred and his bride Tressa Mae. He was born just about the time the Confederate soldiers were making their way to Gettysburg . . . where almost as many Americans would die in a couple of days as would fall in the entire Vietnam War. Tressa was born after the Civil War, right about the time the carpetbaggers were heading south to grab what little wealth was left.

My great-grandfather Fred started out as a plumber's apprentice. He invented the sink trap, but when he showed the concept to his boss he was told to "think less and work more." He abandoned his apprenticeship when he saw the patents for the sink trap appear in his boss's name. I'm not sure whether his choice of a subsequent profession had anything to do with his former boss's actions, but Fred became a butcher. That's what he was doing when he inherited his parents' commercial interests downtown. It was substantial enough that he retired at a young age. Tressa died in 1934, he in '46.

My grandfather Clarence lies here beside my grandmother Theodora. I know of them not from stories in the family Bible or from distant relatives, but from my own childhood. They hold a vivid place in my memories.

Here are a few stones marked "Baby"—children whose legacies were made in heaven.

Over there, across the tombstones, just over a little knoll, you can see the grass where a bronze plate marks my good mother's grave.

Of course, none of the people I've mentioned are actually here in the Kimmel plot. They've all gone on to their destinies. All that's left is a little dust they used to live in and some chiseled names and dates that remind us that they—like us—used to walk and work and wonder and dream.

They had plans and schedules, bills and bank accounts; they laughed and cried; they fought with each other and played together. And, like us, they were watched and followed. Little sets of eyes studied how they treated people—and drew conclusions from what they saw. Sensitive ears listened to their words—and drew conclusions from what they heard. Impressionable minds observed these people from the shadows, sensing the true spirit of their convictions—and drew conclusions from what they felt.

Below the names on these tombstones are epitaphs, marble and granite phrases that try to say in a handful of words what a person's life said over many years.

But true epitaphs are not carved in stone. They are carved in the souls and memories of men and women, boys and girls. Regardless of what my ancestors' tombstones say, the words can never overwrite what those individuals *were*. That's why God leaves the last word on our life to those we leave behind.

Maybe this helps you understand why I like to come out here. It's not some morbid preoccupation with the past. It's perspective. It's a reminder to me that I, too, am going to get my turn at being a memory . . . that I am writing my epitaph now, on the hearts of my children.

They will sum up my life some day. And that sum total will have a deep and abiding effect on the lives that they end up leading.

By the way, how are you doing on writing your epitaph?

We all have to remember that we are not curators of the dead, we are stewards of the living. We are surrounded by the children who must move into tomorrow. Someday we will stand before the God who bought our eternal souls on the cross.

Now we are leaving a legacy. Then we will give an account. Between now and then is all the time that we have left.

We're pilgrims on the journey
Of the narrow road
And those who've gone before us line the way
Cheering on the faithful, encouraging the weary
Their lives a stirring testament
To God's sustaining grace.

Surrounded by so great a cloud of witnesses
Let us run the race not only for the prize
But as those who've gone before us
Let us leave to those behind us
The heritage of faithfulness
Passed on through godly lives.

After all our hopes and dreams have come and gone
And our children sift
Through all we've left behind
May the clues that they discover
And the memories they uncover
Become the light that leads them
To the road we each must find.

Oh may all who come behind us find us faithful
May the fire of our devotion light their way
May the footprints that we leave
Lead them to believe
And the lives we live inspire them to obey
Oh may all who come behind us find us faithful.[16]

A
Legacy
of Love
Weekend Planner

As we have seen, good families don't occur by accident. They are the result of careful planning and deliberate effort. "Parenting on purpose" requires concentrated time in an undistracted setting. One of the best ways to make this happen is for parents to isolate themselves for a weekend in order to work on a strategy. This plan can then be used to develop character traits in their children that will withstand the tests of time.

By getting away at least once a year, a mother and father can evaluate each child's progress, focus on essential character issues, and tailor a strategy that will maximize each child's development over the next year. Weekend planning sessions make legacy-building an easier goal to attain. They provide opportunity to establish goals that can in turn be broken into manageable moments.

To make this process a little easier, I've put together a schedule, some checklists, a few projects, and worksheets to help you get the most out of your weekend. These are designed to help you crystallize your strategy for bringing your children to maturity.

Yes, I realize we all have a built-in aversion to things called "projects" or "worksheets." There's no doubt that a weekend like this will require genuine effort. I'd be lying if I said it would be painless. When we honestly discuss where our children are—and where we are as their parents—it can get frustrating. But your conscientious efforts to develop your family's destiny will put you light-years ahead of most parents, and give you more confidence in where you're going.

This will take an investment of time and money. It will take a commitment to be inconvenienced. But both you and your children will enjoy the reward.

What you have in the pages of this appendix is a suggestion of how you can spend your time. You, of course, know your children's needs better than anyone else. You may need to adapt these projects, or develop some that more particularly meet your needs. What is most important is that you have a *plan*.

God bless you as you build the legacy.

A CHECKLIST FOR A SUCCESSFUL WEEKEND

MONTHS IN ADVANCE . . .

• Pick a weekend and clear the schedule on your calendars.

• Choose an affordable retreat location that provides the comfort, atmosphere, and convenience for a productive weekend.

• Arrange for child care.

• Look over the projects in order to be better prepared to maximize them as a tool for discussion.

• Enlist friends to pray for you during the weekend.

• Pray for a constructive weekend every day for thirty days prior to your retreat.

JUST BEFORE YOU GO . . .

• Pack your Bible.

• Pack family albums, photos of the children, and anything that might help you analyze your children's accomplishments and needs better (report cards, awards, medical reports, counselor's reviews, etc.).

• Pack stationery and notebooks.

• Tell your kids that you are going off to work on next year's strategy for the family.

• Pack your calendars and datebooks. Bring schedules of events that will need to be on the calendar in the following year (work projects, church events, summer camp dates, school calendars, team schedules, etc.).

• Make copies of the projects (you have permission to copy enough to have one to fill in for each child in your family). You may want to use a copier with the capability to enlarge the forms so that you will have more room to write.

SUGGESTED SCHEDULE FOR THE WEEKEND
Friday Evening

The Past:

- Fill in the spaces on Project #1 for each child.

- Spend some time looking at the family album and photos of your children before you go to bed.

Saturday Morning

Quiet Time: See the following suggested Scripture and questions.

The Future:

- Reread Chapter Two: "A Blueprint For Your Child's Character."

- Respond to the information in Project #2.

The Present:

- Begin discussing and filling out the information in Project #3.

Saturday Afternoon

- Complete Project #3.

- Fill in the responses to Project #4.

The Models:

- Work on Project #5 individually.

Saturday Evening

- Put discussions of the kids aside for the evening and enjoy some undistracted time together.

Sunday Morning

Quiet Time: See the following suggested Scripture and questions.

The Plan:

- Work on the suggestions for Project #6.

SATURDAY MORNING'S QUIET TIME

Scripture:

> To the elders among you, I appeal as a fellow elder, a witness of Christ's sufferings and one who also will share in the glory to be revealed: Be shepherds of God's flock that is under your care, serving as overseers—not because you must, but because you are willing, as God wants you to be; not greedy for money, but eager to serve; not lording it over those entrusted to you, but being examples to the flock. And when the Chief Shepherd appears, you will receive the crown of glory that will never fade away.

> Young men, in the same way be submissive to those who are older. All of you, clothe yourselves with humility toward one another, because, "God opposes the proud but gives grace to the humble."

> Humble yourselves, therefore, under God's mighty hand, that he may lift you up in due time. Cast all your anxiety on him because he cares for you (1 Peter 5:1-7, NIV).

1. What advice within this passage stands out in your mind as you consider your role as a parent?

2. What is one promise that you can embrace from this passage to help you through your day?

Pray: For each other, for your children, and for your planning time.

SUNDAY MORNING'S QUIET TIME

What, then, shall we say in response to this? If God is for us, who can be against us? He who did not spare his own Son, but gave him up for us all—how will he not also, along with him, graciously give us all things? Who will bring any charge against those whom God has chosen? It is God who justifies. Who is he that condemns? Christ Jesus, who died—more than that, who was raised to life—is at the right hand of God and is also interceding for us. Who shall separate us from the love of Christ? Shall trouble or hardship or persecution or famine or nakedness or danger or sword? As it is written:

> For your sake we face death all day long;
> we are considered as sheep to be slaughtered.

No, in all these things we are more than conquerors through him who loved us. For I am convinced that neither death nor life, neither angels nor demons, neither the present nor the future, nor any powers, neither height nor depth, nor anything else in all creation, will be able to separate us from the love of God that is in Christ Jesus our Lord (Romans 8:31-39, NIV).

1. What principles within this passage comfort you as you consider your responsibilities as a married couple and as parents?

2. What is a promise that you can claim as you finish up your weekend planning session?

Pray: For your marriage, your children, and your future.

TO GET THE MOST OUT OF THE PROJECTS . . .

• Don't let yourself get bogged down in them. They aren't the final word on your children, nor are they meant to be an in-depth profile of their psychological makeup. They are simply intended as guidelines to help stimulate thought and discussion.

• Feel free to adapt the projects to meet the unique needs of your family and your weekend.

• Notice that some of the projects have a space to list an Action Point for your child. These are specific things that can be done by the child to help develop character, skills, etc. Let me offer a word of caution: When deciding an Action Point for your children, it's essential that you keep in mind that they are *just children.* Their emotions, intellect, bodies, and spirits are young and undeveloped. We parents have an unfortunate tendency to expect levels of maturity and accomplishment from our children that they are incapable of delivering. For instance: In order to build confidence in their faith you might put down as an Action Point that they memorize five chapters from the book of Romans! A far more realistic, enjoyable, and profitable Action Point might be that they memorize five *verses* from Romans. Keep in mind that you have to be prepared to help them through their Action Points.

• Make sure that you complete the Parent's Action Points. These will have more influence on your children than anything you would have them do themselves.

• During your calendar session (Project #6) make sure to schedule three times over the next nine months to review the information on the projects so that you can monitor progress.

PROJECT #1: REVIEWING THE PAST

| Child's Name | Today's Date | Age |

This child's . . .   **This child's . . .**

. . . greatest strengths: **. . . greatest frustrations:**

1. _____   1. _____
2. _____   2. _____
3. _____   3. _____
4. _____   4. _____
5. _____   5. _____

. . . greatest areas of interest: **. . . greatest fears:**

1. _____   1. _____
2. _____   2. _____
3. _____   3. _____
4. _____   4. _____
5. _____   5. _____

. . . greatest accomplishments: **. . . greatest disappointments:**

1. _____   1. _____
2. _____   2. _____
3. _____   3. _____
4. _____   4. _____
5. _____   5. _____

This child's most significant event this past year:

_____

PROJECT #2: FOCUSING ON THE FINISHED PRODUCT

When our children move out from under our authority they need . . .

Decision-Making Skills:

In physical issues (exercise, nutrition, rest, etc.).

In personal issues (finances, career, home life, etc.).

In social issues (dating relationships, love, friendships, dealing with enemies, etc.).

In spiritual issues (dealing with sin, faith, prayer, fellowship, etc.).

Character Traits:

Faith, Integrity, Poise, Discipline, Endurance, and Courage.

Commitment to Life Goals:

To love and obey God.

To love their spouse.

To love their children.

To be a good friend.

To work hard.

To invest their lives in others.

Ability to Execute Survival Skills:

In the physical: manage a schedule, cook, swim, learn safety skills, drive a car, etc.

In the personal: live on a budget, manage a checkbook, know how to finish projects, keep belongings maintained, etc.

In the social: get along with others, confront, resolve, employ good manners, learn to stand alone on an issue if necessary, etc.

In the emotional: to laugh, to cry.

In the spiritual: share their faith, repent, be a friend of God, etc.

Sustained Relationships:

Ability to resolve conflict, serve others, communicate, listen, forgive, etc.

1. Of the skills and character traits mentioned above, which ones do we transfer the most effectively?

_____

_____

2. Of the skills and character traits mentioned above, which ones do we have the most difficult time transferring? Why?

_____

_____

3. What are some of the resources that we can utilize to develop these skills and character traits more effectively in our children?

_____

_____

PROJECT #3: A CHECKLIST FOR MY CHILD'S FUTURE
(Refer to the list in Project #2)

DECISION-MAKING SKILLS	SURVIVAL SKILLS
1.Which skills does he/she use most effectively?	1.Which skills does he/she use most effectively?
2.Which ones need improvement?	2.Which ones need improvement?
Child's Action Point	Child's Action Point
Parent's Action Point	Parent's Action Point
COMMITMENT TO LIFE GOALS	**SUSTAINED RELATIONSHIPS**
1.Which goals are being reached most effectively?	1.Which abilities does he/she demonstrate most often?
2.Which goals need more concentration?	2.Which abilities need improvement?
Child's Action Point	Child's Action Point
Parent's Action Point	Parent's Action Point

PROJECT #4: A REVIEW OF MY CHILD'S CHARACTER

FAITH	How is his/her faith developing? What can we do to help it develop more effectively? He/she deserves a compliment for. . .	**Faith Action Point**
INTEGRITY	How is his/her integrity developing? What can we do to help it develop more effectively? He/she deserves a compliment for. . .	**Integrity Action Point**
POISE	How is his/her poise developing? What can we do to help it develop more effectively? He/she deserves a compliment for. . .	**Poise Action Point**

PROJECT #4: A REVIEW OF MY CHILD'S CHARACTER

DISCIPLINE	How is his/her discipline developing? What can we do to help it develop more effectively? He/she deserves a compliment for. . .	**Discipline Action Point**
ENDURANCE	How is his/her endurance developing? What can we do to help it develop more effectively? He/she deserves a compliment for. . .	**Endurance Action Point**
COURAGE	How is his/her courage developing? What can we do to help it develop more effectively? He/she deserves a compliment for. . .	**Courage Action Point**

PROJECT #5: THE LEGACY OF OUR MARRIAGE
Husband's Worksheet

Three ways that I could demonstrate more faith through my marriage are. . . _____ _____	**Three ways that I could demonstrate discipline before my wife are. . .** _____ _____
One way that I can model faith to the children is . . . _____	**One way that I can model discipline before my kids is . . .** _____
Three ways that I could demonstrate more integrity before my wife are. . . _____ _____	**Three ways that I could demonstrate more endurance through my marriage are. . .** _____ _____
One way that I can model integrity before my kids is . . . _____	**One way that I can model endurance to the children is . . .** _____
Three ways that I could demonstrate more poise through my marriage are. . . _____ _____	**Three ways that I could demonstrate more courage before my wife are. . .** _____ _____
One way that I can model poise to the children is . . . _____	**One way that I can model courage before my kids is . . .** _____

PROJECT #5: THE LEGACY OF OUR MARRIAGE

Wife's Worksheet

Three ways that I could demonstrate more faith through my marriage are. . . _____ _____ **One way that I can model faith to the children is . . .** _____	**Three ways that I could demonstrate discipline before my husband are. . .** _____ _____ **One way that I can model discipline before my kids is . . .** _____
Three ways that I could demonstrate more integrity before my husband are. . . _____ _____ **One way that I can model integrity before my kids is . . .** _____	**Three ways that I could demonstrate more endurance through my marriage are. . .** _____ _____ **One way that I can model endurance to the children is . . .** _____
Three ways that I could demonstrate more poise through my marriage are. . . _____ _____ **One way that I can model poise to the children is . . .** _____	**Three ways that I could demonstrate more courage before my husband are. . .** _____ _____ **One way that I can model courage before my kids is . . .** _____

PROJECT #6: PLANNING THE NEXT YEAR

1. Fill in your central family calendar. Mark all birthdays, scheduled trips, school events, summer camps, team events, church events, etc. Remember to mark down three dates within the next nine months when you will review the worksheets in order to monitor progress.

2. Discuss vacation options and set aside possible dates. Save final decisions until you've sounded out the kids' wishes.

3. Write your children letters on the stationery you brought. You might want to express the reasons why you value them, why you are delighted to be their parents. A few anecdotes from this past year could lend opportunities to tell how you are working to develop their character. You can give the letters to them when you get home, or you may want to save them until the children are older (graduating from college, getting married, when they have their first child, etc.), allowing them to treasure the letters as a gift from their childhood.

4. Review your parent's action points and discuss how and when you will implement them.

5. Put all of the worksheets and projects in files for safekeeping.

6. Pray for your children and each other.

NOTES

Chapter 2

1. Earl Gottschalk, Jr., "Orel Hershiser Sees A Lot of Pitches Related to Money," *Wall Street Journal,* 15 March 1989, 51:1a, 10a.

2. Hal Bodley, "Pete Rose's Kids Throw Some Dirt on Dad," *USA Today,* 23 March 1989, p. 1A.

Chapter 4

3. "Up on the Roof," Gerry Goffin and Carole King, © 1962, 1963 Screen Gems Music Co.—EMI Music Inc. International copyright secured. All rights reserved. Used by permission.

Chapter 5

4. "La Toya Flaunts Her Freedom," *USA Today,* 27 January 1989. Copyright 1989, USA Today. Excerpted with permission.

5. Marilyn Vos Savant, "Ask Marilyn," *Parade,* 18 October 1987, p. 9.

6. Rudyard Kipling, "If," *One-Hundred One Famous Poems* (Chicago: Contemporary Books, Inc., 1958, rev. ed.), p. 113.

Chapter 7

7. Scott M. Peck, M.D., *The Road Less Traveled* (New York: Simon and Schuster, 1978), p. 19.

Chapter 11

8. Russell Dicks, *His Magazine,* cited by Michael Green, *An Expositor's Illustration File* (Dallas: Dallas Theological Seminary, 1982).

9. Anonymous author.

10. Adapted from Dr. Louis H. Evans, *Marriage Prayer for Bride and Groom.* Used by permission.

Chapter 13

11. Dennis Conner with Bruce Stannard, *Comeback—My Race for the America's Cup* (New York: St. Martin's Press, 1987), pp. 65-66. Used by permission.

Chapter 14

12. Ann Landers, *Los Angeles Times* and Creators Syndicates. Used by permission.

Chapter 15

13. "The Living Years," Mike Rutherford/B. A. Robertson, ©1988 Michael Rutherford Ltd./R & BA Music Ltd./Hit & Run Music (Publishing) Ltd. Administered by Hidden Pun Music, Inc. (BMI) for USA. International copyright secured. All rights reserved. Used by permission.

14. Charles R. Swindoll, *Come Before Winter,* (Portland, Ore.: Multnomah Press, 1985), p. 233.

15. Major General Courtney Whitney, *MacArthur: His Rendezvous with History* (Westport, Conn.: Greenwood Press, Publishers, 1955), p. 100.

Epilogue

16. "Find Us Faithful," Jon Mohr, © 1987 Birdwing Music/Jonathan Mark Music (Administered by The Sparrow Corporation, P. O. Box 2120, Chatsworth, Calif., 91311). All rights reserved. International copyright secured. Used by permission.